Mazda MX-5

THE COMPLETE STORY

OTHER TITLES IN THE CROWOOD AUTOCLASSICS SERIES

Mazda MX-5

THE COMPLETE STORY

ANTONY INGRAM

THE CROWOOD PRESS

First published in 2013 by
The Crowood Press Ltd
Ramsbury, Marlborough
Wiltshire SN8 2HR

www.crowood.com

British Library Cataloguing-in-Publication Data
A catalogue record for this book is available from the British Library.

ISBN 978 1 84797 496 9

Acknowledgements
This book would not have been possible without the assistance, time,
enthusiasm and kindness of the following people: Martin Dooner,
proprietor MX5 City, Doncaster; Phil Marks and the team at Milcars
Mazda, Watford; all at Elstree Aerodrome, Radlett; Alison Terry at Mazda
Motors UK; and Pete Kent, Kendra Evans, Caroline Bennett and Kurt
Ernst for sharing their MX-5-related thoughts. Apologies to those who
I've missed – I guarantee your help has been appreciated. Further thanks
go to all my friends, family and colleagues for their support and patience.
This book goes out to those who only put the hood up when it rains!

Designed and typeset by Guy Croton

Printed and bound in India by Replika Press Pvt Ltd

CONTENTS

INTRODUCTION

Cars like the Mazda MX-5 don't come around very often. Not sports cars specifically, of which there are plenty and always have been to some extent. One might argue, in fact, that the concept of an open-topped two-seater is as old as the car itself, even if much has changed since the late 1800s.

Nor is the MX-5 a rare car in numbers. Quite the opposite; many an owner will regale you with the MX-5's inclusion into the *Guinness Book of Records* as the world's best-selling roadster. As open-topped cars go, they are prolific.

No, the MX-5's rarity is in combining such talents that it becomes more than just a device for moving between A and B, though it is undoubtedly as competent as any other vehicle for doing just that – which makes it even more of a rare object. Thousands upon thousands of drivers use their MX-5s on a daily basis, in all weathers and for all purposes. That it can do this, as well as serving as a car to be driven solely for fun, while retaining such a reputation for reliability, makes Mazda's diminutive sports car very special indeed. That it is merely one sports car among many, or that its popularity has risen above that of any other sports car ever

produced, are simply sidelines to a story of a car designed by genuine enthusiasts but appreciated by everyone. Some sports cars have very limited appeal, but the MX-5 works because it attracts all manner of owners – enthusiasts, racers, older buyers wishing to rekindle memories of MGs and Triumphs from their youth, and younger buyers looking for their first taste of fun motoring. Or none of the above – buyers who might simply wish for a stylish, reliable runaround – and the MX-5 covers all these bases.

Proof that this formula works is easy to find. The MX-5 is almost a household name and, at the very least, one of the more recognisable shapes on the road. The earliest models, over two decades old, have become modern classics, while the later models are still as usable as the average hatchback, yet all share the same distinctive silhouette, and are distinctive as being from the same line.

The following pages will cover the story of the Mazda's history, through the first, vestigial ideas, to production and beyond. Building an icon isn't easy, but it is rewarding and the MX-5, known as the Miata in the Americas, an old German word for 'reward', is a reward we can all share.

The 1989 Mazda Eunos Roadster – the Japanese market MX-5. MAZDA (BOTH)

MAZDA MX-5 TIMELINE

1979, February: Journalist Bob Hall talks with Mazda's Kenichi Yamamoto about developing a classic 'bugs in the teeth' sports car

1981, May: Mazda opens US research and development facility in Irvine, California

1983, January: Bob Hall and designers Fukuda and Yagi, start initial design sketches for the new roadster project

1984, January: Design teams in Japan and the US start working on three competing design, front-drive, rear drive and mid-engined

1984, August: American design – front engine, rear drive – is chosen

1984, September: Development work begins in Hiroshima

1985, September: IAD tests development prototypes tested at MIRA in the UK

1986, April: Masaaki Watanabe and design team begin to sketch final proposals for the MX-5

1986, August: Final technical decisions made, rotary engine discounted

1987, April: Plastic-bodied prototype previewed to public

1987, September: Final MX-5 design approved

1988, April: US journalists drive a prototype in Japan

1989, February: Production begins, car shown at Chicago Auto Show

1989, September: First deliveries of both base model and Special Package Eunos Roadsters are made in Japan

1990, March: Automatic transmission option added to the Eunos Roadster range

1990, May: First European customers receive MX-5s

1990: Brodie Brittain Racing develops turbocharged MX-5

1991, June: Mazda wins Le Mans 24 hours, releases special edition orange and green MX-5 in celebration

1992, November: 250,000th MX-5 produced

1993, December: 300,000th MX-5 produced

1994, March: MX-5 gains 1.8-litre engine and chassis tweaks

1995: Reduced-output 1.6 MX-5 re-introduced as a budget option

1998, March: Second-generation MX-5 unveiled at the Geneva Motor Show

1999, January: Mazda celebrates MX-5's 10th anniversary with 7,500 of a special edition model. Sold worldwide, they are all blue, with blue interior detailing

1999, February: Half a million MX-5s produced. 500,000th car is a gold Mk2 with a tan roof

2000, May: 531,890 MX-5s produced, new Guinness World Record for open-top, two-seat roadsters

2000, December: 600,000th MX-5 produced

2001, January: MX-5 facelifted, known as 'Mk2.5'

2003, October: Mazda launches fixed-roof coupé MX-5 in Japan; never sold overseas, and only built to order

2005, March: MX-5 Mk3 goes on sale

2005, April: 700,000th MX-5 produced

2005, November: Mazda Roadster voted 2005-2006 Japan Car of the Year – first victory for Mazda in 23 years

2006, July: MX-5 Roadster Coupé launched, first MX-5 with retractable hard top

2007, January: 800,000th MX-5 produced

2009, May: MX-5 Mk3 receives facelift, known as 'Mk3.5'

2009, July: 20th anniversary of MX-5 celebrated in Japan with special edition

2010, February: 875,000th MX-5 produced

2010: 20th anniversary of MX-5 sales in the UK celebrated with special model, based on 1.8-litre car

2011, February: 900,000th MX-5 produced

CHAPTER I

MAZDA BEFORE THE MX-5

The company now known as Mazda was established as Toyo Cork Kogyo Co. Ltd in 1920, in the city of Hiroshima, Japan. Its name was changed to Toyo Kogyo Co. Ltd in 1927, before manufacturing of machine tools began in 1927. A new factory was opened in Hiroshima during 1930, before production of the company's first vehicle, a three-wheel utility truck called Mazdago, began in October 1931.

Toyo Kogyo began exporting these trucks to China early the following year. It continued producing tools and vehicles for the next decade and a half, until Hiroshima was devastated by the American atomic bomb attack in

1945, which brought about the end of the Second World War. Toyo Kogyo avoided the blast and the Hiroshima prefecture office used its facilities until July 1946. Exports restarted in 1949, when the company began sending its three-wheel trucks to India.

From 1960 Toyo Kogyo produced more and more vehicles, beginning with its first passenger vehicle, the Mazda R360 Coupé. The sporty R360 was a four-seat coupé powered by a 356cc air-cooled engine developing 16hp. More than 4,000 units had been sold by the end of 1960, the car's low price bringing car buying within reach of the average worker.

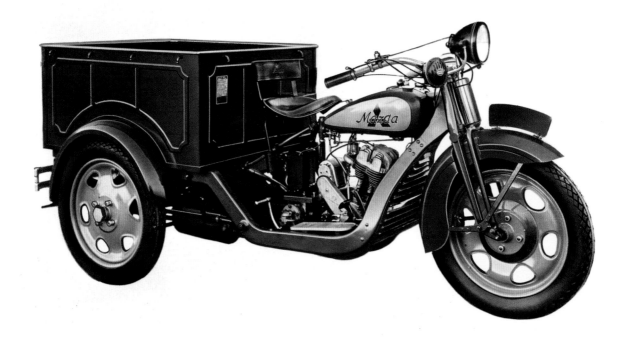

The very first Mazda – a three-wheel delivery trike. MAZDA

Mazda's R360 Coupé became the first in a long line of sporting vehicles from the company. MAZDA

The Mazda Cosmo 110S became a highly respected sports car in Japan. It marked the starting point of Mazda's affinity with the rotary engine. MAZDA

The RX-7 nametag is associated with one of Mazda's most famous lines. Lightweight and nimble handling made the original a match for the contemporary Porsche 924. MAZDA

The company made another important move in 1961, joining forces with German auto maker NSU on development of rotary engines, a type of engine that became synonymous with Mazda over the following decades, even as interest from other manufacturers – notably Citroen and NSU – waned. The French company dropped the concept after making only a small number of production rotary-engined models, while NSU was hit by warranty claims for failing engines and was eventually absorbed into Audi. Meanwhile, four-door passenger vehicles followed the R360 and as Mazda passed its first million sales, it started the Familia line of family cars.

The company's interest in rotary-engined vehicles finally produced a car in 1967, with launch of the Mazda Cosmo Sports 110S. The Cosmo developed 110hp from its twin-rotor engine, easily breaking the 100mph (161km/h) barrier and racing down the quarter mile in just 16.3 seconds. Developments the following year gave the car 128hp and a top speed of 200km/h (124mph), with even greater acceleration. The pretty and futuristic 110S became a company milestone, and set a tone for sports car development at Mazda that continues to the present day.

From here, the company developed rapidly. US exports began in 1970, and over the next few years Mazda released a line of other rotary-powered vehicles, carrying the now familiar 'RX' tag. The first RX-7 hit the market in 1978, beginning a line of rotary sports cars that continued well into the 2000s. Produced until 1985, the first-generation RX-7, known as the FB in enthusiast circles, used a 12A, twin-573cc rotor engine developing 128hp at 7,000rpm. The car benchmarked the recently launched Porsche 924, but with a rotary engine and acres of velour and vinyl covering its interior, it could only be Japanese in origin.

Ford Association

Mazda entered into a financial tie-up with the Ford Motor Company in 1979, before officially becoming the Mazda Motor Corporation in 1984. The second-generation RX-7 sports car arrived in 1985, with power increased to 146bhp and offering more torque from its larger twin-rotor engine. Now mimicking the Porsche 944 in style, but again treading its own path in driving experience, the new

Mazda won the 24 Hours at Le Mans in 1991 with the 787B. MAZDA

car meant that Mazda could now be taken seriously as a producer of sports cars.

By the time the third generation RX-7 – the beautiful and curvaceous 'FD' – arrived in 1991, the MX-5 was already becoming a global sales success. The FD is consistently rated highly by enthusiasts and critics alike, and was one of a handful of Japanese sports cars that shocked the West out of its complacency towards Far-Eastern cars. Both Japan, and particularly Mazda, had arrived on the sports car big time.

Mazda's sporting line-up continued to grow throughout the 1990s, aided by its historic victory in the 24 Heures du Mans, using the rotary-powered 787B. To this day, the 787B's Le Mans win is both Mazda and Japan's only victo-

ry in the 24-hour event, and the only victory for a rotary-powered car.

Mazda launched the MX-3 coupé in 1991, featuring one of the world's smallest production V6 engines, and the larger MX-6 in 1987, developed in conjunction with Ford, to join the MX-5 and RX-7. Japan's home market was gifted the tiny AZ-1 kei-class sports car in 1992 to compete in Japan's smallest car class, and with these models and others, Mazda became renowned for its sporting models and unique engineering. It is a reputation that continues and is proudly promoted by Mazda with its 'Zoom-Zoom' slogan, which is used worldwide. Reviews of Mazda's more humdrum models regularly note that its cars seem infused with MX-5 DNA – yet another legacy of the MX-5's development.

CHAPTER 2

CONCEPTION

The Sports Car Market

As Europe began to get back on its feet and prosperity improved following the Second World War, several European car manufacturers began developing simple, lightweight sports cars using mechanicals from their more mundane offerings. It became a market segment that endured for decades, since the average buyer on an average wage could happily find themselves behind the wheel of something far more fun and exciting than the usual saloon car offerings. This sports car buzz boomed in the 1960s, a period often considered the golden age of the sports car. Britain and Italy led the way, developing cars like the MGB, Triumph Spitfire, Alfa Romeo Duetto and Fiat 124 Spider, all of them simple to drive and maintain, and inexpensive to produce.

Then, in 1975, a team of engineers at Volkswagen developed a car that would change motoring completely. Just one year earlier, the German manufacturer, better known for its rear-engined Beetle, had shocked the market with the front-engined, front-wheel driven Golf hatchback. But 1975's Golf GTI took the concept further.

Here was a car that demanded no compromises from its user. One could walk into a Volkswagen dealership and purchase one of the most practical cars on the market, but also one that would shame many a sports car in the all-

Kenichi Yamamoto, father of the rotary engine and instrumental figure in the MX-5's conception.
MAZDA

14

important traffic light Grand Prix, further humiliating them in the corners. It went, steered and stopped like a sports car, but the roof didn't admit a drop of water in a downpour, and the boot could hold a week's worth of shopping. With fuel injection, it even started every morning. And for the teams tasked with designing a performance car that people could use every day, putting a large engine into a platform that had already been developed and paid for many times over, made far more financial sense than developing an expensive, rear-drive sports car entirely from scratch.

These were characteristics that the humble sports car could not hope to offer. The sports cars of the time were being further compromised by burgeoning emissions and safety regulations, making them slower and heavier, and compromising their styling with large, impact-absorbing bumpers. Had the Golf GTI remained the sole 'hot hatchback' on the market, then this may not have been such a problem for the few remaining sports cars, but soon other car manufacturers caught on to the concept of selling souped-up shopping cars and over the next decade these affordable, fun and practical vehicles decimated what was left of an increasingly struggling sports car industry.

It is ironic, then, that less than a year later than the Golf GTI's debut at the Frankfurt Motor Show, the seeds were being sewn for a motoring revolution of a different kind, and one whose fruits would not be seen for another thirteen years.

The Seeds are Sown

In early 1979, Bob Hall, a motoring journalist at American magazine *Motor Trend*, had a meeting with Kenichi Yamamoto and Gai Arai, head of research and development at Mazda. Before he left, Hall mentioned to Yamamoto that he thought Mazda should be producing a lightweight sports car. A big fan of 1960s' British sports cars, but irritated by their quality issues, Hall became enthusiastic about a modern version. The company already had the rotary-powered RX-7 on its books, but Hall was looking for something simpler, lighter and cheaper.

While the concept went down well with Yamamoto, Mazda's top brass would need more persuading to enter a market that seemed to be moving further and further away from lightweight roadsters. The project began to gain momentum in the early 1980s, when Hall met with some of

Bob Hall – The journalist who conceived the MX-5

'Any greatness and longevity the MX-5 has is based primarily in the car's purity and simplicity of concept.'

Without Bob Hall, there would likely be no Mazda MX-5. Not only that, but the 1990s' small sports car boom may also never have happened, and the concept of a cheap performance car would be very different today. It was Hall's desire for a sports car that rekindled the spirit of the 1950s and 1960s, without resurrecting their foibles, which led to the world's greatest-selling roadster.

Back in 1996, American motoring journalist Hall was writing for *Motor Trend* magazine, and it was his meeting with Kenichi Yamamoto and Gai Arai that kicked off the MX-5's development. Speaking to Don Sherman at *Automobile Magazine*, he recounted his first conversations with the Japanese engineers.

'I shifted into overdrive. I babbled at 70mph (in a trans-Pacific hodgepodge of English and Japanese) how the RX-7 is a neat car, an A-plus sports car, but the simple, bugs-in-the-teeth, wind-in-the-hair, classically British sports car doesn't exist anymore. I told Mr Yamamoto that somebody should build one…'

The rest, as they say, is history. In 1981, Hall joined Mazda as part of the team that would develop the MX-5, eventually launched in 1989. Hall has now moved on from Mazda, living and working out in Malaysia for Proton, as head of product planning and programme engineering.

the RX-7 development team at the famous Pebble Beach Concours d'Elegance, held in Monterey, California. Mazda lead designer Shunji Tanaka happened to mention words that would come to embody the concept throughout its development – 'lightweight sports car'. Provided the car remained light, it would influence the entire driving experience. This was backed up in a study by Mazda North America Operations, which stipulated that a suitable sports car would need to be light, seat only two people, have exciting styling and use a front-engined, rear-drive layout.

Although no development was done, Hall had planted a seed that would steadily grow over the decade. In 1983, a meeting with Mazda designer Shigenori Fukuda allowed Hall to reiterate his desire for a simple sports car, leading Fukuda to set up the unusually-titled 'Off-line, Go Go' project. This encouraged Mazda's design and engineering staff to create a new small sports car. Hall was taken with the project and joined Mazda's North American product planning and research division. Yamamoto was then promoted as President of Mazda Motor Corporation and finally able to give the concept the backing it needed. Along with designers Tom Matano and Mark Jordan, Hall and Fukuda worked on early proposals for a new sports car – the beginning of the project to create 'Mazda eXperimental-5'.

Several designs were proposed as part of the 'P729' programme, a code for the roadster project. To this end, a selection of various clay models was produced. A competition was held within Mazda, to test the water for potential sports car concepts. Three teams worked on different drivetrain layouts – one a traditional front-engined, rear-drive sports car, the next a simple, front-engine, front-wheel drive layout and the final proposal a more radical mid-engine design. Front-drive was becoming popular, since it was simpler to engineer and build, improved cabin space and allowed for plenty of flexibility in terms of engine choice.

The mid-engined design was also strongly considered, since the front-drive engine and drivetrain could easily be adapted. While both front-drive and mid-engine options would allow Mazda to reduce the amount of bespoke engineering required, it became increasingly clear that to develop a sports car that stayed true to their original vision, a front-engine, rear-drive layout was required. This concept, developed by the team at the Mazda North America base in Irvine, California, became the basis of the project.

The team also worked on different body proposals, even debating whether the new car should be a traditional convertible, or a fixed-roof coupé. The car's design was the subject of much heated debate within Mazda, and several designs were initially suggested. Gradually, the MX-5's now-familiar shape was formed, refined and tweaked with each new model. The engineers had even coined a phrase to describe the car's ethos, the now oft-repeated 'Jinba Ittai' – 'oneness between horse and rider'. The term stemmed from old Japanese culture and accurately described the level of connection that drivers would feel behind the wheel of the new car. Even by this stage in the model's development however, Mazda was still unsure on whether to push forward with further design and research. It was still in doubt as to the car's potential market, given the changing tastes of the time's consumers.

Early MX-5 development sketches, with obvious 1980s' styling cues.
MAZDA

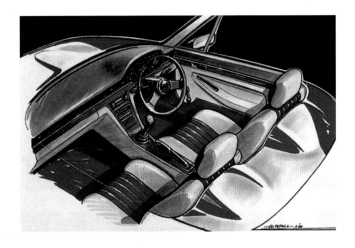

The interior design shows a more conventional layout than the production version. MAZDA

This sketch includes some of the MX-5's well known smoother lines. MAZDA

This interior is close to the final production version. MAZDA

Here the gear lever has a Ferrari-style open gate. Sadly, it's something that didn't make production. MAZDA

One of the early Californian prototypes. The styling has a little way to go before it arrives at the production configuration. MAZDA

By April 1987, Mazda had built a full-scale plastic-bodied prototype of one of the design proposals. It presented it to 220 members of the US public, to gauge their reaction. The reception was positive, with fifty-seven participants going as far as to say they 'would definitely buy it if it hit the market'. This reaction to the car in the world's biggest automotive market reassured Mazda that such a project was viable. Five months later, the design was finalised.

By this point, engineering evaluation work had begun at International Automotive Design (IAD) in Worthing, Sussex. The concept car and prototyping specialists had been tasked with replicating the feel of an old British sport cars, with everything from the chassis and steering to the exhaust note, taking inspiration from those classic British vehicles. Meanwhile, personnel changes at Mazda had delayed the project a little, before Shunji Takana, Mazda's senior designer in Japan, was transferred to Irvine, California. Takana's eventual redesign actually brought the prototype's looks much closer to the original version created by Hall, Matano, Jordan and Fukuda.

As the design was finally signed off, work began on the suspension and drivetrain. Mazda had selected a four-cylinder 1,597cc unit from the contemporary Mazda 323 GTX, a turbocharged hatchback with which Mazda was having some success in Group A rallying. To the iron block, Mazda fitted a new aluminium cylinder head with double overhead camshafts and four valves per cylinder. This allowed the car to rev smoothly to high engine speeds, so a 7,200rpm electronic limiter was installed. Shorn of forced induction, the strong unit was re-tuned for better throttle response and a classic exhaust note, the latter being one reason for ditching the turbocharger – Mazda felt it would mute the classic sports car noises. Multi-point fuel injection was also fitted for optimum combustion and better fuel consumption, and new camshafts were fitted to improve top-end power.

It was attached to a five-speed manual gearbox lifted from the Mazda 929, the feel of which was again tuned to evoke a classic sports car experience – the engineers called for a shift that could be operated by the mere flick of a wrist. Mazda also worked on what it termed the

Kenichi Yamamoto – Head of Research and Development at Mazda, 1979

'I really would like the next generation to be unafraid of making mistakes and to maintain a spirit of challenge.'

As with Bob Hall, without Kenichi Yamamoto and his colleague Gai Arai, there would be no MX-5. Perhaps equally significant for Mazda, there would also be no rotary-engined Mazdas, for Yamamoto-san had been with Mazda since the early days and played a part in every rotary-engined model that ever left the Hiroshima factory.

Born in Kumamoto, Yamamoto-san graduated from Tokyo University in 1944, after majoring in machinery. During the war he manufactured aircraft and joined the Toyo Kogyo company after the war ended.

During his work with Toyo Kogyo, the company which preceded Mazda, he began work in the rotary engine (RE) research department, the team set up to develop Mazda's version of Felix Wankel's rotary engine. Initially, Yamamoto wasn't taken by the idea. 'No way!' he recalled, in a 1998 interview with the *Chugoku Shimbun*, a Hiroshima newspaper. 'Reciprocating engines have a history of almost 100 years, and it is not easy to develop a new engine.'

Despite this, and concerns that a small company like Mazda should not be attempting something that large companies such as General Motors and Ford had not, the project went ahead. In 1967, the team produced the Mazda Cosmo 110S, a rotary sports car. Other rotary models followed, and 1978 marked the launch of the first RX-7. Since then, Mazda has been synonymous with Wankel rotary-engined cars, and has achieved success that their original proponents, NSU and Citroen, could only dream of.

And then, in February 1979, Yamamoto-san and Gai Arai talked with Bob Hall about the sort of cars Mazda should be producing. As Yamamoto-san rose up Mazda's ranks to eventually become president, he was able to help make Hall's vision happen. That car is the MX-5, and its legacy has arguably even outlasted Mazda's rotary efforts.

Mazda designed a special double overhead cam cylinder head for its 1.6-litre engine. ANTONY INGRAM

The clean, elegant lines of the early Mk1 MX-5 look as good today as they ever did.
PETE KENT // @NOTPOSHPETE

'Power Plant Frame', a structure that rigidly connects the transmission and differential, preventing torque from the rear wheels twisting the chassis, and improving both the feel and response of the drivetrain.

The suspension was far more sophisticated than anything else at this level in the market, since RX-7 engineer Takao Kijima had insisted on an unequal-length double-wishbone set up, front and rear. While the suspension was advanced, the interior was simple, the work of interior designer Kenji Matsuo. The engineers' ethos of Jinba Ittai was applied throughout the car's development, reducing weight and complexity wherever possible. The long bonnet was to be of aluminium to reduce weight and improve the front-to-rear balance and even unseen components, like the exhaust, were carefully considered, stainless steel eventually used to improve gas flow. The roof was yet another concession to Jinba Ittai. A powered roof was initially considered, but rejected on the grounds of weight and complexity. A manually operated soft top was ultimately chosen, one which drivers could raise and lower from their seat in a matter of seconds.

With safety an increasing factor in many markets, the team also used the relatively young technique of computer analysis to develop a body that was as strong as it was light, without the compromises on styling that had afflicted its 1970s and early 1980s predecessors.

By 1988, Mazda already had twelve prototypes up and running. In July of that year, the American press was let loose in the car to gauge opinion. Their verdict, unsurprising to those who have driven the MX-5 in the years since, was 'build it!'

Not without reason, news of the MX-5's development was starting to attract the attention of the motoring press. A 1988 issue of *Autocar & Motor* carried the headline 'Sports Car War!', with Mazda taking the fight to rival sports cars from Lotus – the M100 Elan – and Ford, with a 'new Capri' that ultimately disappeared, never to be seen again.

Mazda's position was also unusual as the only manufacturer pursuing a rear-wheel drive layout. The Lotus Elan was the first front-drive Lotus sports car in the company's history and Ford's stillborn Capri would also have been front-wheel drive. It didn't take long for the press and the car industry to realise Mazda's retro intentions. Quotes from industry observers noted that Mazda had bought examples of old British sports cars, like the MGB, Triumph Spitfire and Lotus Elan, pulling them apart and examining their smallest details in an effort to recreate them in a more modern form. It would also allow Mazda to iron out any shortcomings found in the classics, while retaining their appeal.

Magazines noted the MX-5's Elan-like styling – ironic, given the totally new direction taken with the contemporary Elan. The 21 December 1988 issue of *Autocar & Motor* carried spy photographs of the car, shortly before its Chicago show debut. 'Our photographs show a little car with undeniable good looks... the car uses lots of soft contours and rounded lines in a subtle revamp of the old Coke bottle style.'

The writing was on the wall for other makers, there being little doubt in the eyes of critics that Mazda had taken the right route with its reinvention of the classics.

CHAPTER 3

MAZDA MX-5 MK1 (NA)

MARKET LAUNCH

When the MX-5 finally hit the Mazda stand at the Chicago Auto Show on 10 February 1989, Mazda was prepared to find out if all those years of planning and development had been worthwhile – and the press would find out whether sports cars still had a place in the world.

The MX-5 certainly had all the correct ingredients. The rounded 1960s' profile and delicate details were in stark contrast to most 1980s' cars; few manufacturers had started to introduce the curvy shapes that would dominate for the next decade. The size and proportions too were from another era, and the car must have looked tiny next to the Chicago show's other stars that year, the Chevrolet Corvette ZR-1 and Dodge Viper concept.

Pop-up headlights were a definite nod towards the original Lotus Elan, though their electric action was swifter and considerably more reliable. The classic Lotus had also influenced the rounded front grille and pert tail. Beneath the bonnet, even the cam cover had more than an element of Lotus Twin Cam about it. Mazda openly admitted that several old British sports cars had influenced the MX-5, but Colin Chapman's classic was certainly the most flattered by Mazda's imitation.

The wheels were a combination of retrospective and modern, too. Their seven spokes had more than a hint of classic British Minilite alloy wheel about them, though the 14in alloys were actually created for Mazda by Japanese wheel specialist Enkei. More than just a styling feature, the wheels were also incredibly light, reducing un-sprung weight, to the benefit of handling. Enkei later supplied other wheel designs for the MX-5, its products appearing on several special editions.

Key Rival: Toyota MR2 (1984–1989)

Toyota's 'Mid-ship Runabout, 2-seater' was already in the twilight of its life when Mazda released the MX-5, but had almost single-handedly carried the small sports car through its 1980s 'rough patch' of hot hatchback domination. With echoes of the earlier, Bertone-styled Fiat X1/9, the Toyota's tiny profile and sharp lines gave it an almost origami appearance.

Inside, the square-edged shapes continued, in a complete contrast to the retro-styled MX-5 but, like the Mazda, it was the Toyota's driving experience that won people over. Toyota's famed 4A-GE four-cylinder engine sat between the cabin and rear axle. With 128bhp it was more powerful and revved harder than Mazda's 323-sourced 1.6, and a tiny 950kg (2,094lb) kerb weight ensured sprightly performance. The handling was as sharp as the styling – less forgiving than the Mazda, but for some enthusiasts, even more incisive and rewarding.

Pricing would be key to the Mazda's success, of course. In North America the MX-5, badged Miata, kicked off at just $14,000 and when it finally arrived on UK shores in 1990, at a little under £15,000 it had the market virtually to itself. The severely outdated, but sub-£10,000 Fiat X1/9 had been killed off the year before and even its more modern equivalent, Toyota's MR2, had abandoned the lightweight concept. Its replacement, endowed with Ferrari-esque looks and a £15k price tag for the basic model, had little more power than the MX-5, but considerably more weight.

Released with just three colour options on its launch in the UK, the MX-5 in traditional sports car red became very popular.
ANTONY INGRAM

Compact and simple, the MX-5 was quickly recognised as a classic design. ANTONY INGRAM

The original seven-spoke alloy wheels were soon nicknamed 'daisies', for obvious reasons. They were designed to evoke the distinctive Minilite wheels of many British classic cars.
ANTONY INGRAM

As for the British sports cars that Mazda had paid such flattering homage to, few remained. Lotus had launched the Elan M100 in 1989, but dumbfounded many with the decision to go front-wheel drive. The M100's 'wedge-of-cheese' styling was not to all tastes either, though it at least came with pop-up headlights, in a nod to its forebear. Caterham's Super Seven fulfilled the sports car brief somewhat, but as a usable, every-day proposition it ranked lowly.

There were other British challengers too, but none were as accessible as the MX-5. Morgan offered the Plus Four and TVR the S2. The former was keenly priced, but its old-fashioned looks and build were ever-present to scare off a wider audience, and the latter was quick, frail and very low volume – in production, if not aural terms.

In fact, the Mazda's real competitors were the hot hatchbacks that had effectively killed off the MX-5's inspirations all those years before. People had become used to the concept of unlikely performance from a familiar hatchback body and the practicality – not to mention warmth and dryness in poor weather – of the hot hatch had made sports cars obsolete.

This put the new MX-5 up against some tough competition. Volkswagen was fielding the second generation of its Golf GTI, now available with a 16V engine, offering greater performance than ever. Ford still sold the inexpensive Escort XR3i, Fiat the Uno Turbo and Japanese rival Honda offered the quirky CRX. Most were cheaper than the MX-5, but none offered wind-in-the-hair motoring, nor did they offer the purist driver the enticing option of power-oversteer.

Mazda didn't expressly mention this in its launch brochure of course, though a gratuitous image of the car in a long, sideways drift around a skidpan did find its way in. These, of course, were days in which openly demonstrating you'd made a fun car wasn't yet politically incorrect.

Early reception

What Mazda did openly claim was that 'the sports car is back!' The brochure heavily promoted all the features that you just could not get from your average hot hatchback. If there was any compromise in only having two seats or little luggage space, the driving experience would surely make up for it.

With a kerb weight of 955kg (2,105lb), the MX-5 had all the virtues of low mass that Colin Chapman had been

extolling since the 1960s, meaning its modest engine, brakes and tyres had relatively little work to do. Performance from the 1,598cc inline-four could never be considered fast (despite Mazda's claims of 'superb performance'), but it was enough to ensure the car was fun and the motor was happy to be taken all the way to the red line. Even if it did not provide the outright speed of some of its hot hatch rivals, the MX-5 did very well at providing the impression of speed.

Just before you hit the limiter, the engine gave its maximum 114hp at 6,500rpm and a rasp from the exhaust, strongly reminiscent of those sports cars of yore. You had to work hard for your 100lb ft of torque too, which was reached at 5,500rpm. The under-stressed, 323-derived engine was always tractable, so driving at lower speeds was never a chore. The MX-5 could even be encouraged to return decent fuel economy; 30mpg (9.4ltr/100km) certainly wasn't out of the question, and on longer cruises, over 40mpg (7.1ltr/100km) was within reach.

A snappy, close-ratio gearshift made the playful performance easy to access too. Contemporary road tests considered it one of the car's best features and quickly propagated one of road testing's greatest clichés – 'a rifle-bolt gear change'. With perfect clutch and throttle pedal weighting, drivers were encouraged to change gear more than was strictly necessary, just to enjoy the mechanical interaction between their hand and the inner workings of the gearbox.

The steering too was a delight to use. Many drivers had been brought up with front-wheel drive and had become accustomed to the feeling of the front tyres being tugged to-and-fro during acceleration or cornering. With the Mazda, steering efforts were unsullied by power and a kerb weight spread evenly between the axles contributed to the need for only a light input to 'aim' the car.

The superlatives flowed from magazines across the globe. *Autocar & Motor* was particularly full of praise. 'It is its ability to involve the driver in its every reaction that makes it such a joy,' it wrote in its March 1990 road test. 'Few others, at any price, can offer so much.' *Car & Driver* in America was even more succinct. 'We felt like cheering,' it said, after driving the car.

Mazda had decided, perhaps influenced by the car's simple construction, that only basic features were needed in the cockpit, and this attracted one of the few press criticisms about the original car. Many felt it was a little too

Japan and America – Eunos Roadster and Miata

Of course, the MX-5 wasn't just limited to Europe and the Japanese market –the huge interest from America proved vital to its success. Known as the Mazda Miata, it joined a market where competition was scarce and quickly became a hit.

Aside from the change from right- to left-hand drive, the MX-5 recipe for America was the same as the UK and European models. Tiny detail changes were made including the addition of a small boot-lid brake light, a feature shared with the Japanese market versions. The rear number plate recess was also changed, to suit America's square licence plates. Inside, the US model was also available with an airbag right from the start, so American customers were denied the pretty Momo steering wheel enjoyed by their European and Japanese counterparts. Further revisions included a passenger airbag, which made the dashboard considerably more bulky and spoiled the interior's minimalist feel.

There were no such problems in Japan. Mazda had launched the MX-5 under the new Eunos sub-brand, which focused on the more specialised vehicles in its range and later included the V6-engined MX-3 sports coupé and the luxurious Xedos 6 and Xedos 9 saloons.

Known simply as the Eunos Roadster, it had a much more generous specification than the UK and US models. For the enthusiast driver, all 1.6 Roadsters were equipped with a viscous limited-slip differential, increasing traction and allowing greater control in cornering. Different engine mapping liberated a few more horsepower too, bringing the total to 120bhp.

A basic model was available with steel wheels, manual windows and no power assistance for the steering, but further up the range specification was higher than that in other markets. Air conditioning was standard on higher-spec models, and the cloth seats were equipped with headrest speakers.

Another option denied to the UK market, some might say thankfully, was automatic transmission. Fitted with heavy Japanese traffic in mind, it was a particularly basic four-speed unit, actually derived from the transmission found in London taxis. Performance and economy lagged behind that of the manual versions, but it did add an extra dimension to the MX-5 experience. For those who valued styling and ease of use above sports car handling and control, the automatic was a welcome addition.

CLOCKWISE FROM TOP LEFT:
Eunos models feature different badging to their European counterparts. ANTONY INGRAM

Eunos Roadster models often have different interior trim, such as this stainless steel speaker surround. ANTONY INGRAM

Roadster badging marks this car out as a Japanese import. ANTONY INGRAM

Basic, dark and sombre, the MX-5's interior never quite won the praise granted to its exterior. ANTONY INGRAM

The small 'eyeball' vents may look inadequate, but they are more than up to heating the small cockpit, even with the roof down.
ANTONY INGRAM

basic and colourless, with simple – but comfortable and durable – cloth seats, and black plastic as far as the eye could see.

The centre console was uncomplicated and the dash punctuated by four circular air vents and the curved instrument binnacle, which housed simple and usefully clear chrome-ringed dials, another homage to those old British sports cars. Kinder road testers described it as 'no-nonsense', though it was certainly one area of the car that drew less praise overall.

Spartan it might have been, but Mazda ensured the basics were right. For shorter drivers at least, the driving position was perfect. The seat was mounted low and perfectly aligned with the steering wheel and pedals, the sales brochure even boasting that the pedal layout encouraged heel-and-toe gear-changes. The gearshift, beloved by testers, was easy to access and mounted a matter of inches from the steering wheel rim. For taller drivers the seat was mounted a little too high and some found the open convertible top a necessity just to fit inside the car.

Early models lacked an airbag, but featured a sporty three-spoke Momo steering wheel with a padded centre. Many owners quickly realised that this could be removed to reveal the wheel's metal spokes and Allen-head bolts, giving more of a motorsport feel to the cabin.

Those same owners might also have wondered how to access the fuel filler for that first refuelling stop – Mazda had seen fit to hide the tiny filler door handle in a cubby between the seats, under a padded cover was handy for resting the elbow during longer journeys. When the roof was up, the large shelf behind the seats could be used for carrying larger items as a supplement to the boot, which was compromised by its need to house both the battery and the space-saver spare wheel.

Perfect Weight Balance

The reason for this oversight in practicality was to endow the MX-5 with another true sports car attribute – perfect weight balance. Mazda's engineers had worked hard to ensure an even weight distribution between the front and rear axles, and moving the 9kg (20lb) battery to the boot had helped achieve this target, as well as freeing space in the engine bay. The engine itself was situated just aft of the front axle line and to further remove weight from the front of the car, the large front bumper was made of plastic.

To keep overall weight down, a major component providing chassis strength was also from aluminium, just like the bonnet. Known as the Power Plant Frame, it was a girder-like structure connecting the gearbox and differential through the transmission tunnel, with the propshaft running down the middle. It was designed to minimise chassis flex and vibration from torque reaction, allowing the car to transmit its modest power to the road more effectively.

The Power Plant Frame didn't quite stop the dreaded scuttle shake though. Hard cornering forces and bumps in

A simple cabin and an even simpler hood – just right for enjoying brief moments of sunshine. MAZDA

the road encouraged the chassis of many open cars of the time to flex and shudder. The MX-5's scuttle shake was by no means terrible by the standards of the day, but noticeable compared to the relative stiffness of closed-cockpit cars and it was among the few complaints of the press.

Another, at least from some quarters, was aimed at the car's ride quality. Certain roads not only induced scuttle shake, but could also set the little Mazda pitching and bobbing, and sharp bumps would send a shudder through the cabin. Many felt this a price worth paying to maintain that class-leading handling.

More than anything else, the Mazda's unique selling point was its ability to drop the roof in a matter of seconds, via two plastic clasps atop the windscreen frame. This could be done while seated, the cabin's compactness meaning the passenger clasp could still be reached by the driver.

Erecting the hood was a little trickier, but more supple drivers could still achieve this from their seat. Whether they would want to or not having often experienced their first taste of open-air motoring would be another matter. Just as the MGB had back in the 1960s, the MX-5 brought open-top motoring to a wide range of drivers and the UK's temperate climate ensured that many owners 'went topless' as often as possible. An efficient heating system – something many of those early British sports cars lacked– also meant that top-down driving in winter was no longer out of the question.

A relatively aerodynamic shape ensured that even with the roof down, wind buffet wasn't severe, particularly with the side windows raised. Conversing with a passenger actually became possible, without the need for raised voices. Top-down driving was further encouraged as a way of hearing that classic exhaust note.

Perhaps even more importantly, and very much unlike the MGB, Midget, Spitfire, Elan, and all the MX-5's other inspirations, Mazda had spent a great deal of time and effort to ensure the hood fitted perfectly – making leaks in poor weather a thing of the past. Owners could be confident of leaving the car outside on a wet day or driving in torrential rain, yet still arriving at their destination with dry clothes.

For perhaps the first time, an inexpensive sports car had become a true all-year-round proposition. Hot hatchbacks had killed off small sports cars in the 1980s, but Mazda was now giving them a dose of their own medicine.

The early Mk1 MX-5 has a simple, timeless shape.
ANTONY INGRAM

Compared to modern cars, the MX-5 is surprisingly compact.
ANTONY INGRAM

An open road and an MX-5 is a combination too tempting for some to resist. ANTONY INGRAM

Technical Specifications, MX-5 Mk1

Mazda MX-5 1.6i (1989-1993)

Layout and chassis
Two-seat open-top sports car, steel monocoque, steel and plastic panels

Engine
Type: Mazda, four-cylinder inline
Block material: Cast iron
Head material: Aluminium
Cooling: Water
Bore and stroke: 78 x 83.6mm
Capacity: 1597cc
Valves: Four valves per cylinder, 16 in total, DOHC
Compression ratio: 9.4:1
Carburation: Multi-port electronic fuel injection
Maximum power (DIN): 114bhp at 6,500rpm
Maximum torque: 135Nm (99.5lb ft) at 5,500rpm
Fuel capacity: 45ltr (9.9Imp gal)

Transmission
Gearbox: Mazda 5-speed manual, all synchromesh
Clutch: Single dry plate
Ratios   1st 3.136:1
          2nd 1.888:1
          3rd 1.330:1
          4th 1.000:1
          5th 0.814:1
          Reverse 3.758:1
Final drive: 4.300:1

Suspension and Steering
Front: Independent double wishbones, gas-filled dampers
Rear: Independent double wishbones, gas-filled dampers
Steering: Rack and pinion, hydraulic power assistance optional
Tyres: 185/60 R14
Wheels: Aluminium alloy, 14in
Rim width: 5.5in

Brakes
Type: Ventilated discs front, solid discs rear
Size: 234mm (9.2in) front, 231mm (9.1in) rear

Dimensions
Track
Front: 1410mm (55.5in)
Rear: 1428mm (56.2in)
Wheelbase: 2266mm (89.2in)
Overall length: 3948mm (155.4in)
Overall width: 1676mm (65.9in)
Overall height: 1224mm (48.2in)
Unladen weight: 955kg (2,105lb)

Performance
Top speed: 195km/h (121mph)
0-62mph: 8.8 seconds

Mazda MX-5 1.8i (1993-1998)

Layout and chassis
Two-seat open-top sports car, steel monocoque, steel and plastic panels

Engine
Type: Mazda, four-cylinder inline
Block material: Cast iron
Head material: Aluminium
Cooling: Water
Bore and stroke: 83 x 85mm
Capacity: 1840 cc
Valves: Four valves per cylinder, 16 in total, DOHC
Compression ratio: 9:1
Carburation: Multi-port electronic fuel injection
Maximum power (DIN): 132bhp at 6,500rpm
Maximum torque: 155Nm (114lb ft) at 5,000rpm
Fuel capacity: 45ltr (9.9Imp gal)

Transmission
Gearbox: Mazda 5-speed manual, all synchromesh
Clutch: Single dry plate
Ratios   1st 3.136:1
          2nd 1.888:1
          3rd 1.330:1
          4th 1.000:1
          5th 0.810:1
          Reverse 3.758:1
Final drive 4.100:1

Suspension and Steering
Front: Independent double wishbones, gas-filled dampers
Rear: Independent double wishbones, gas-filled dampers
Steering: Rack and pinion, hydraulic power assistance optional
Tyres: 185/60 R14
Wheels: Aluminium alloy, 14in
Rim width: 5.5in

Brakes
Type: Ventilated discs front, solid discs rear
Size: 234mm (9.2in) front, 231mm (9.1in) rear

Dimensions
Track
Front: 1410mm (55.5in)
Rear: 1430mm (56.3in)
Wheelbase: 2266mm (89.2in)
Overall length: 3975mm (156.5in)
Overall width: 1676mm (65.9in)
Overall height: 1224mm (48.2in)
Unladen weight: 990kg (2,182lb)

Performance
Top speed: (197km/h) 122mph
0-62mph: 8.2 seconds

Brodie Brittain Racing Turbo

If one of the few criticisms of the MX-5 at launch was its relative lack of power, then turbocharged conversion offered by Brodie Brittain Racing (BBR) in 1990 was the perfect antidote. Officially sanctioned by Mazda UK, customers could actually walk into their local Mazda dealership and place an order for the red-hot upgrade, which raised the basic 1.6's power from 114 to 152bhp, produced at the same 6,500rpm. The conversion also gave the car more than 50 per cent more torque, at 209Nm (154lb ft).

Performance was given a useful boost, the quoted 6.8 second 0–60mph sprint was over two seconds quicker than the standard car could manage, and top speed now touched 130mph (209km/h). The kit was a thorough one, with several modified components replacing Mazda's original parts, including an uprated exhaust manifold and down-pipe, a modified sump, uprated hoses, an air-to-air intercooler and modified power steering, water and oil-system pipe work in the more crowded engine bay. The centrepiece was a water-cooled Garrett T25 turbocharger, offering around 850 lucky owners the chance to have the fastest MX-5s on the road.

If even the 68-piece turbocharger kit wasn't enough, buyers could also specify options such as uprated suspension, alloy wheels, a rear spoiler and a limited-slip differential kit. The conversion was so thorough that Mazda even offered a 3-year, 60,000-mile warranty with every car sold, giving buyers extra peace of mind.

The increasing popularity of the early MX-5s led BBR to release an updated and improved turbocharger package in 2011, at a cost of £7,500. Garrett still supplies the turbocharger, now a GT25 ball-bearing unit, and with an air-to-air intercooler and 'piggy-back' ECU (engine control unit), the modern kit adds over 100bhp to the original 1.6, with a power output of 220bhp. Torque is raised to 237Nm (175lb ft). As well as the engine upgrades, the package essentially turns the customer's MX-5 into a new car, with rust treatment, a full re-spray, new seats, larger wheels and tyres, and a suspension package.

BBR Mk3

Now known as BBR GTi, the company hasn't only worked its magic on the Mk1 cars. Modifications for the Mk3 and Mk3.5 MX-5s are becoming increasingly popular, and the company has developed tuning parts and forced-induction kits that raise performance to significantly higher levels.

September 2012 saw the launch of the BBR Super 180 upgrade. Rather than turbocharging or supercharging, the Super 180 upgrade is a package of naturally aspirated tuning to raise power of the 2.0i models from 158bhp to 180bhp at 6,800rpm. The car also sees improved torque output throughout the rev range, with 27Nm (20lb ft) extra torque at its 4,250rpm peak.

BBR GTi fits a new stainless steel 4-into-1 exhaust manifold, a 2.5in (16mm) stainless steel exhaust centre section with a high-flow catalytic converter and centre silencer, and a new back box, with 3.5in (89mm) tailpipes. A BBR high-flow panel air filter and StarChip ECU remap complete the changes, BBR claiming to improve both driveability and throttle response in the process. Even the upgraded exhaust is designed to avoid producing unnecessary noise, so just as with original BBR conversions, the car should remain driveable every day. Customers can even specify the package for the 1.8i cars, and while maximum output is less than that of the 2.0-litre models, power and torque gains are similar.

There are always customers who want more though. For them, the BBR-Cosworth Stage One and Stage Two packages turn the MX-5 into a car to worry high performance BMWs and Porsches. Cosworth's decades of experience in engine building have helped conceive a supercharger package for both 1.8 and 2.0-engined MX-5s, liberating as much as 258bhp from the latter.

The Stage One package consists of a Cosworth and BBR-designed inlet manifold, an Eaton MP62 supercharger, air-to-water intercooler, high-flow injectors, a new airbox and filter, upgraded hoses and fixings, and a BBR StarChip remap. Power of the 1.8 models rises to 217bhp – 93bhp greater than standard, while Mk3 and Mk3.5 2.0-litre cars rise to 235 and 241bhp, respectively, the latter thanks to the Mk3.5's raised rev limit. Torque increases by over 68Nm (50lb ft) on all versions.

Stage Two takes the tuning even further, as BBR also fits many of the components of the Super 180 package – a stainless exhaust manifold, a new stainless steel exhaust centre section with high-flow cat and silencer, a new BBR-branded back box, high performance air filter and Stage Two ECU remap. Tests on the dynamometer show an increase of 107bhp on the 1.8, which reaches 231bhp in total. Mk3 and Mk3.5 cars become even more potent, the latter reaching 258bhp, with 282Nm (208lb ft) of torque.

Now, as it was more than two decades ago, BBR is still capable of turning something fun into something fierce. For the handful of customers who have always felt the MX-5 has lacked a little performance, tuners like BBR could be just the solution.

An original BBR Turbo MX-5.
MAZDA/BBR

With BBR's skill in turbocharging and Cosworth engine components, the BBR Cosworth is a frighteningly quick take on the Mk3 MX-5.
BBR RACING

The BBR Super 180 offered a little more power for sports car fans. BBR RACING

1993 – First revisions

However perfect a car may seem at launch, the passage of time sees trends change and allows the competition to catch up, so in 1993 Mazda launched an updated MX-5.

Sensibly, it refrained from dabbling in a facelift, and some new wheel designs aside, the MX-5 remained the retro masterpiece that had won so much praise when it had first appeared on the motor show stand in Chicago. Nor had they spent too much time altering the interior. With the exception of a new and particularly ugly airbag

steering wheel – thankfully available only as an option at launch – the same simple shapes and dark trim remained.

The seats had been revised, now incorporating separate, adjustable head restraints, more suitable for taller drivers. The seat bases were also made a little deeper to help accommodate a wider range of driver sizes. The hood mechanism was as simple as ever and luggage space equally as compromised.

The revised range offered three options. Topping these, Mazda offered a new 1,839cc engine option, lifted from the Mazda 323F GT. With a 14hp and 14Nm (10lb ft)

ABOVE AND OPPOSITE: *The MX-5's similarity to the 'Frogeye' Sprite is obvious when the headlamps are raised, while from the back, there's more than a hint of Lotus Elan.* ANTONY INGRAM

torque advantage over the old 1.6 (now a maximum of 152Nm/112lb ft at 5,000rpm), the 1.8 was not introduced to increase the car's performance, but instead to offset a weight increase across the range, a result of several strengthening bars for the chassis and some new safety options. Weighing as much as 1040kg (2,293lb), the 1.8 was now 70kg (154lb) up on the original car.

Ensuring the new 1.8-litre car stopped as well as it went, Mazda upgraded the brake discs, fitting larger 255mm (10in) diameter discs at the front and 251mm (9.9in) discs at the rear – both 20mm larger than on the original car. Further increasing safety, Mazda equipped the car with side impact bars, previously only found in the Japanese V-Special edition, as standard.

Two versions of the 1.8 went on sale. Most popular was the 1.8iS, a top-specification model with a long list of standard equipment and some significant changes over the original MX-5. In addition to body strengthening, taking the form of under body brace bars and another just behind the seat backs, the 1.8iS also offered anti-lock brakes and a driver-side airbag – both necessary safety measures in an increasingly safety-conscious market.

1.8iS models also came with alloy wheels, electrically adjustable door mirrors, electric front windows, power-assisted steering and a high-mounted third brake light, now standard across all markets. That third brake light, as well as an engine immobiliser, could also be found on the other two new MX-5s, the 1.8i and 1.6i.

Mariner Blue was a popular colour on early MX-5s, and it's still among the most distinctive today.
PETE KENT // @NOTPOSHPETE

These models were the new, more budget-conscious options. The 1.8i was mechanically identical to the 1.8iS, but shorn of much of its equipment – the electric mirrors and windows, ABS and driver's airbag all disappeared from the equipment list. Visually, the 1.8i also lacked the higher-spec model's alloy wheels, using utilitarian, 14in steel rims instead.

This made it difficult to tell apart from the cheapest new MX-5, the 1.6i. With the 1.8 now occupying the same performance bracket as the old 1.6, the new car could cater for a different area of the market – those less concerned about performance, but still taken in by the MX-5's attractive shape.

With only 90hp, the 1.6i lacked the performance of the new 1.8 or the old 1.6. Officially, it could complete the 0-62mph sprint in 10.6 seconds, or two seconds slower than Mazda claimed for the 1.8. It also topped only 175km/h (109mph), to the 1.8's 198km/h (123mph) top speed. With lower performance, Mazda also retained the smaller brakes fitted to the older 1.6, with 235mm ventilated discs

It isn't difficult to spot Austin-Healey and Lotus influence in the MX-5, particularly in the pop-up headlights. ANTONY INGRAM

at the front, compared to the 1.8's 255mm discs, and 231mm solid discs at the rear.

There were fewer changes elsewhere, all cars sharing the same five-speed manual gearshift, 2.8-turn lock-to-lock steering ratio and identical dimensions inside and out. Initially, power steering was left off the 1.6-litre cars, but soon became a standard fit for customers who preferred their driving to be a little less physical.

The MX-5 continued to win over public and press alike. Road testers found that the marginal increase in weight over the first cars was an acceptable compromise, given the increase in power and torque of the 1.8-litre engine. Many also noted the rigidity and ride quality benefits associated with Mazda's tweaks to stiffen the chassis.

Autocar & Motor praised the new base models in particular, despite criticism of the new steel wheels, which it described as 'less than pretty'. More positively received was the lack of unnecessary items like electric mirrors and windows, and central locking. Testers reasoned that none added to the driving experience, but the absence of

The rear lights are simple and attractive. Changing bulbs is easy. ANTONY INGRAM

Tsutomu 'Tom' Matano – Designer, MX-5 Mk1

'It [the MX-5] started out as our own little indulgence of what we wanted to have.'

Tom Matano is often described as the 'father of the MX-5'. Born and raised in Japan, his design career kicked off at the Los Angeles Art Centre of Design, where he attained a Bachelor's Degree in 1974. He subsequently moved to General Motors, before joining Mazda in 1983, to work on the MX-5 project with other designers including Mark Jordan, Wu Huang Chin, Norman Garrett and Koichi Hayashi.

Following the success of the original MX-5, Matano stayed with Mazda for several years, leading the Mazda international design organisation and being one of the team responsible for the 'Zoom-Zoom' line-up in 1999 and 2000.

In more recent years, Matano has worked on his own design projects in San Francisco, as well as becoming Executive Director at the Academy of Art University's School of Industrial Design. Matano is still seen around the MX-5 scene on occasion. Most recently, he spoke with Bob Hall, Garrett, and Jordan at the inaugural 'Miatafest' in Irvine, California, a festival to celebrate the MX-5's 20th anniversary.

He described the MX-5's conception as a rare moment of clarity. 'All elements clicked in Japan and the US. We pressed the issue at the right moment, and we had a great team.'

The tan hood and British Racing Green paintwork of the V-Spec make for a traditional British sports car look.
ANTONY INGRAM

these items did not harm the ownership experience either. Even the lack of power steering did not prove a problem, one tester commenting that the slightly slower steering rack – 3.3 turns lock-to-lock – was still quick enough to catch any slides an owner might indulge in. Nor was it too heavy, provided you were travelling above 32km/h (20mph). The hood was still praised for its simplicity, but the interior still criticised for a lack of flair and colour, though few criticised the driving position, which remained ideal for most body shapes.

Nevertheless, by 1997, a full eight years after its launch at the Chicago Auto Show, the Mk1 MX-5 was starting to get a little long-in-the-tooth; not for how it drove, so much as by the standards of refinement and performance

expected in the class. Several rivals had joined the fray since its introduction, including Fiat's pretty and sprightly Barchetta, based on a Punto platform, and MG's latest contender, the MGF.

The BMW Z3 had also made a splash. Although it was aimed at a more upmarket audience with larger, straight-six engines, a less-powerful 1.9-litre four-pot was also on sale, very clearly aimed at potential MX-5 customers who might be swayed by the more aggressive lines and prestige appeal of the BMW badge. Mazda needed a new competitor, one that could match its emerging rivals on performance, cosset drivers with a more modern interior, and still retain the handling magic that had ensured its success over the last eight years. Step forward, the MX-5 Mk2.

CHAPTER 4

DRIVING A MK I MX-5 TODAY

With the earliest examples of the Mazda MX-5 now over twenty years old, drivers might expect the car to feel old-fashioned. After all, technology has moved on at quite a rate and even basic 'shopping' cars offer performance and comfort not far removed from that of larger family cars in the 1980s. Sports cars now offer significantly increased performance, and even the MX-5 offers bigger engines with higher power outputs.

One thing that hasn't aged is the MX-5's styling. The soft, rounded lines have not always been kind to the Mazda, encouraging 'hairdresser's car' stereotypes in the UK and 'chick's car' stereotypes in America, arguably from those too macho to appreciate the subtler aspects of car styling.

To everyone else, the shape is still as pert and simple as it ever was. From whichever angle a driver approaches, the MX-5 is still a great looking vehicle, endowed with all the popular classic sports car cues that drew people in more than two decades previously. The side profile still has the right proportions, with a long bonnet leading into that curved, Elan-inspired nose. With the pop-up headlights raised, the car trades chic for cheeky and has a hint of Austin Healey 'Frogeye' Sprite about it, but when lowered they endow the front end with uncluttered looks that later versions of the car have never really matched.

An MX-5 and an empty road – what more excuse do you need to go for a drive? ANTONY INGRAM

There are subtle curves everywhere, from the discreet bulge in the aluminium bonnet, to small flares in the wheel arches, to the slight lip in the boot lid, a line slightly spoiled by the third brake light incorporated with the car's facelift in 1993.

The smaller details also stand the test of time, including the tiny, chromed door handles. Though not the most practical means of entering the car, and although the chrome on older cars is prone to pitting, they look less clumsy than the standard plastic units in later MX-5s. The retro-style wheels look small by today's standards, and at 14in diameter they genuinely are small, but visually they lend a classic feel to the car. Constructed from low-weight aluminium, they're also functional.

The retro look continues when the lightweight bonnet is lifted, with the Lotus-style cam cover and engine pointing north-south, in keeping with the front-engined, rear-wheel drive format. Compared to modern engine bays, some may find it cluttered, but it is mechanically simple and components are easy to access for maintenance and modification, which is not always the case with the acres of plastic under the bonnet in new cars.

Plastic is more prevalent on the interior. Modern interiors have stepped up in quality and design, but the MX-5 offers a simple environment in keeping with the car's character. The plastics are simple but effective and stand the test of time in higher mileage examples, a testament to Mazda's quality control standards. Enlivening the otherwise dark interior and dashboard are chrome-ringed speedometer and tachometer dials, flanked by water temperature and fuel level gauges, with an oil pressure gauge sitting at the top, reading in PSI. There are simple warning lights dotted around, but few will see them illuminated, given the MX-5's reputation for reliability.

The centre console contains two small, round air vents. They don't look capable of emitting much air, but as MX-5 owners will happily regale, they can be surprisingly effective, even in colder weather. Between the vents is the hazard warning switch, and a button that allows you to raise and lower the headlights without turning them on, which is useful for changing bulbs. Below these are simple controls for the heating and fans, and a double-DIN space for the radio. If a smaller unit is used, half of this space is becomes a handy oddment tidy. Another storage tray sits between the seats, along with the electric window switches. Inside the centre cubby you'll find the fuel door release.

The seats are comfortable and well shaped, with a better mounting position for taller drivers in post-facelift cars. The steering wheel sits perfectly in line with the driver's seat, with the pedals slightly displaced to the right due to the wide transmission tunnel – though less offset than in the latest generation of MX-5.

The short, stubby gearstick, beloved of owners and motoring journalists alike, is just a palm's width from the steering wheel. The handbrake initially feels like it is

Tiny chrome door handles were among the MX-5's most beautiful features. ANTONY INGRAM

Everything you need and nothing you don't, the cabin is flair free and functional. ANTONY INGRAM

Clear dials abound – rev counter, speedometer, fuel gauge, oil pressure gauge and coolant temperature. ANTONY INGRAM

Owner's view: Kendra, Yorkshire
Mk1, Merlot Edition

Kendra is no stranger to MX-5s – her late Merlot edition is the third she's owned, and a Mk2.5 in Splash Green is likely to follow at some point. She bought the Merlot in August 2012 for the same reason as the others. 'I love the sheer 'chuckability' of them… there is never a dull moment when driving one, yet they can be as exciting or refined as you like.' While Kendra is yet to buy her first Mk2, it was a Mk2 that provided her first taste of MX-5 motoring. After driving one for the first time, she was hooked. 'I had an absolute hoot in it!' While the Merlot is standard, future MX-5s may not stay that way for long – 'The great thing about Mk1 and Mk2 MX-5s is that you can add forced induction really easily… the addition of a turbocharger or supercharger makes a brilliantly fun car even more fun!'

mounted a little too far to the left, but drivers quickly adapt and it might impede quick gear changes if mounted any closer.

The engine fires instantly with a turn of the key, sending a momentary judder through the car before settling into a high, but smooth idle. The little oil pressure gauge needle works its way towards 60PSI from cold, settling down to around 30PSI at idle when warm. The responsive throttle sends the pressure needle upwards, with the tachometer doing likewise. There's a distinctive rasp from the exhaust and a slight rock from the chassis as the engine reciprocates.

On the Move

On the move, the car feels alive – small movements of the steering send it to and fro, even if directly around the centre position it initially feels a little dead. The engine is anything but, those quick revs when stationary translating to eager responses out on the road. With the engine warm, indicated by the water temperature gauge reaching the halfway mark, drivers can begin to explore the performance. MX-5 owners will happily tell you their car is not the quickest vehicle on the road, but they'll also confirm that

it rarely matters. The engine is smooth and responsive all the way through the rev range and gear changes can be made with incredible economy of movement using that tiny gear lever. When the engine and gearbox are still cold, changing gear takes a little more effort, and sometimes requires a careful change between first and second. Modifications from 1993 onwards made this a smoother affair. When warm, the change is slick and satisfying, a perfect complement to the characterful engine.

By modern standards the brakes feel a little weak, but pedal feel is excellent and the hard pedal feels natural underfoot. The wheels can lock under heavy braking – no ABS on the early MX-5s – but this takes significant effort. Judged by the rest of the car though, the brakes work well, their power is matched to the modest power from the engine and the relatively low levels of grip.

The 185-profile tyres don't offer much outright grip, but the benefits far outweigh the downsides. For a start, when the tyres finally do break traction at relatively low speeds, resulting slides are easy to handle, whichever end of the car loses grip first. Turn in a little too quickly and you'll be presented with understeer, but a small lift on the throttle lets the nose dig back into the tarmac. In dry weather, drivers find they have to be brutal with the throttle or aggressive with the brakes and steering wheel to provoke oversteer, but once again it's easy to control with a little lift, some correction from the steering, or a combination of the two.

In the wet, drivers pressing on a little harder will find it easier to break traction at the rear – surprisingly so, sometimes, but no less easy to correct. Take a bend at moderate pace in second or third gear, and a squeeze on the throttle will see the rear tyres breaking away relatively quickly. While this is fun for the more experienced driver, it can come as a bit of a shock for some and it is not unusual to find used MX-5s with rear panel damage. Keen drivers will find that the car will hold a sweet, easily-controlled drift until they let off the gas again, or until the open differential spins its power away through the inside wheel and the car corrects itself.

MX-5 drivers will recount how they always feel so connected with the car that moments like this soon become second nature. Unlike many modern sports cars, there's never enough power to intimidate (nor huge reserves of grip to overcome), so drivers feel capable of exploiting the car's potential more often. With so much of its talent accessible at thoroughly sensible speeds, licence-losing

Cheeky pop-up headlights were a nod to British sports cars of the 1960s and 1970s. ANTONY INGRAM

Only a clumsily placed fog light spoiled the lines at the back of UK cars. ANTONY INGRAM

velocities are more difficult to attain than in the current crop of powerful sports cars.

The original MX-5 works on other levels too. It may be rough and ready when pushing on, but driven at a more sedate pace, its other qualities shine through – surprising mechanical refinement, light steering and lower noise levels than some expect. It is a car that's equally happy doing a weekly shop (albeit a small one, for no more than the two people one can fit in its cockpit), as it is on a scenic Sunday drive, or flat-out around a racetrack.

This, of course, is what has endeared so many people to the model. While forgiving on the limit for drivers wishing to explore the finer points of vehicle control, it remains a fun car to drive for those with no interest in driving, and at lower speeds there's rarely any risk of losing control. Its compact dimensions make it easy to park and wieldy in city driving, but it is also as comfortable and reliable as any supermini.

Then, when the mood and the weather allows, owners can drop the top in seconds and revel in one of the most primal driving sensations, that of uninterrupted headroom, the rush of wind, and all the sounds and smells normally locked out of regular cars. Cars may have advanced since the MX-5 first hit the market, but the pleasures available in driving an early example are no less relevant than they were two decades ago – and at so little money these days, perhaps even more so.

CHAPTER 5

MAZDA MX-5 MK2 (NB)

The second generation of MX-5, with the chassis code NB, broke cover at the Tokyo Motor Show in 1997. Though largely based on the platform of the car that preceded it, its external appearance had matured beyond the retro look of the original. The original MX-5 had lasted an incredibly long time with relatively few changes. Most car models have a five or six-year product cycle, with a refresh half way through. But the enduring appeal of the MX-5 Mk1 had ensured it stayed on the market for a whole nine years and sold more than 580,000 units, with only modern comfort and safety requirements prompting an update. Changes were still relatively few, Mazda's

designers and engineers not wishing to play too much with a winning formula.

Early details of the revised car revealed that its dimensions were little removed from those of its predecessor, a by-product of using the same chassis. Styling tweaks had been limited to give what the press described as a 'more muscular, fatter look'. Every panel was new, apart from the windscreen surround, which in early spy shots was painted black, rather than the body colour of production cars.

Some 95 per cent of the styling work was carried out at Mazda's design centre in Los Angeles, with the remaining details changed by Hiroshima's designers. Early reports

This early proposal for the Mk2 MX-5 was more retro than the finished product, but still used fixed headlamps. MAZDA

An unusual shade of gold paint, suiting the car's more curvaceous styling, was popular on early Mk2 MX-5s. MAZDA

suggested that Mazda had worked hard to remove Ford influences from the front end, since the two companies were working together on other projects at the time but Mazda wanted the MX-5 to be all its own. Aside from any influence emanating from Ford, Mazda's component suppliers had also been shown the Rover Group's MGF, the popularity of which was increasing in Europe and may have influenced the new MX-5's design direction.

What Mazda could not deny was that many of the changes had been implemented in order to save money. Even after the final design of the Mk2 had been signed off, Mazda was still holding meetings in order to discover ways of reducing the unit cost of each vehicle. Weight too was discussed, since changes including a larger fuel tank, extra safety equipment and body strengthening had resulted in a car weighing more than 1000kg (2,205lb) in early prototypes, a figure that rose higher with production.

In terms of styling, the new car had a softer, more flowing look. Taking inspiration from Mazda's own RX-7, which had gained beautiful curves through the 1990s, the aluminium bonnet was more sculpted than on the old model, and the front wings were taller and more flared – much more Jaguar E-Type than Lotus Elan. The doors were less rounded than before, and the pretty but impractical chrome door handles were replaced by cheaper, more conventional units. Most noticeable of all, Mazda had dropped the pop-up headlamps. In their place were simpler (and cheaper) almond-shaped units, meaning the car's aerodynamics were now unaffected at night. Mazda actually noted that the new lamps gave the front end a cuter look, something that would increase the car's appeal even further with women.

The pop-up headlamps had gone, but the Mk2 MX-5's styling was more mature than that of its forebear. HAYMARKET MEDIA GROUP

The engine bay of a Mk2 1.6i. HAYMARKET MEDIA GROUP

A Mk2 MX-5 1.6i in silver. HAYMARKET MEDIA GROUP

The Mk2's interior had also grown up. An airbag was now standard and equipment levels were higher. *HAYMARKET MEDIA GROUP*

Boot space was improved by moving the spare wheel and battery beneath the boot floor. *MAZDA*

The rear wings had also become more voluptuous, the curves now flowing into the arched boot lid. This incorporated a third brake light, a feature familiar to the Japanese and American markets and introduced on later European Mk1 cars. The body had also been strengthened, with thicker sills, a thicker floor frame and reinforcements that improved torsional rigidity by 6 per cent. The body changes resulted in a car slightly larger than its predecessor and 40kg (88lb) heavier.

Mazda also made changes in the cabin. The basic layout of the controls remained unchanged, but the design was updated to late 1990s' tastes, with more curves, more up-to-date heating controls and an increase in the quality of materials.

All models now featured driver and passenger airbags as standard, the driver's unit inside a Nardi-designed three-spoke steering wheel. The dials were similar to those of the first-generation car but now used an italic script, and all versions also lost the chrome rings found on Mk1s. Mazda had worked hard to maintain the 'retro' feel of the original cabin, but a new curved upper section to the dashboard, now with integrated air vents, brought the materials and design up to date.

The sliding heater controls were replaced with rotary units, and the centre console now featured a digital clock and a bank of switches. Further improving the driver's experience in the cabin, Mazda finally fitted a glass rear screen, replacing the previous plastic screen, which was prone to fogging. Engineers also found 20ltr (0.7Cu ft) more boot space – up to 144ltr (5.1cu ft) – by moving the spare wheel and battery out of the boot and down to bumper level – the spare wheel under the car and the battery beneath the boot floor.

Despite the visual changes and interior modernisation, Mazda had stuck to the old principal of 'if it ain't broke, don't fix it' as far as the mechanicals were concerned. Both the 1.6 and 1.8-litre engines of the later first-generation cars were carried across to the Mk2, albeit in states of increased tune to make up for the increase in weight.

Basic 1.6-litre cars crept up from only 90bhp in the later Mk1 cars, to 110bhp. Torque was increased to just under 134Nm (99lb ft). The power of the 1.8-litre unit went up from 128bhp to 140bhp, and there was 161Nm (119lb ft) of torque at 4,500rpm. Just as with the final Mk1 cars, Mazda understood that buyers of the more powerful 1.8-engined car would be more likely to appreciate a torque-sensing limited-slip differential, and those opting for the

Milestone – MX-5 Number 500,000

On 8 February 1999, Mazda produced its half-millionth MX-5 roadster – nine years and ten months after the very first MX-5 rolled off the line. Mazda still owns the car, a Samba Gold Mk2 with a beige hood and beige interior. The company later submitted the milestone to Guinness World Records for verification. It was confirmed a few months later.

less powerful 1.6 would not mind going without.

The 1.8 models also benefitted from standard-fit anti-lock brakes, and 15in alloy wheels. The 1.6 cars had steel wheels as standard, but many buyers upgraded to alloys, in keeping with the MX-5's stylish character. Buyers of the 1.6 cars also missed out on the 1.8's wider track and thicker stabiliser bars, fitted to improve handling on the more powerful model.

Some subtle engineering changes had also improved torsional rigidity, with the use of more body reinforcements, while the styling tweaks had reduced aerodynamic drag – the Mk2's coefficient of drag had dropped to 0.36 from the Mk1's 0.38.

Other features offered as standard on the 1.8 models included electric windows and mirrors, while a more attractive Nardi airbag steering wheel was featured in the top-spec 1.8iS. Indeed, the Mk2 MX-5 was a significantly better-equipped car than its predecessors, ensuring it remained competitive against its new found rivals in the marketplace.

Reception

Though not quite the revolution that the original car had been back in 1989, the advent of a new generation of MX-5 was still a big deal, and coverage in the motoring press was widespread. Much of it was positive. Reviewers understood that the MX-5 had needed to grow up, even if that involved losing some of the character of the outgoing model. The clean new lines went down well, and few mourned the loss of the pop-up headlights – the new units gave the car a more mature look, and did not affect its aerodynamics at speed.

Technical Specifications, MX-5 Mk2

Mazda MX-5 1.6i (1998-2003)	Mazda MX-5 1.8i (1998-2003)

Layout and chassis

Two-seat open-top sports car, steel monocoque, steel and plastic panels

Engine

Type: Mazda, four-cylinder inline
Block material: Cast iron
Head material: Aluminium
Cooling: Water
Bore and stroke: 78 x 83.6mm
Capacity: 1597 cc
Valves: Four valves per cylinder, 16 in total, DOHC
Compression ratio: 9.4:1
Carburation: Multi-port electronic fuel injection
Maximum power (DIN): 108bhp at 6,500rpm
Maximum torque: 134Nm (99lb ft) at 5,000rpm
Fuel capacity: 50ltr (11Imp gal)

Transmission

Gearbox: Mazda 5-speed manual, all synchromesh
Clutch: Single dry plate
Ratios　1st 3.136:1
　　　　2nd 1.888:1
　　　　3rd 1.330:1
　　　　4th 1.000:1
　　　　5th 0.814:1
　　　　Reverse 3.758:1
Final drive 4.300:1

Suspension and Steering

Front: Independent double wishbones, gas-filled dampers
Rear: Independent double wishbones, gas-filled dampers
Steering: Rack and pinion, hydraulic power assistance
Tyres: 185/60 R14
Wheels: Aluminium alloy, 14in
Rim width: 5.5in

Brakes

Type: Ventilated discs front, solid discs rear
Size: 234mm (9.2in) front, 231mm (9.1in) rear

Dimensions

Track
Front: 1405mm (55.3in)
Rear: 1430mm (56.3in)
Wheelbase: 2266mm (89.2in)
Overall length: 3975mm (156.5in)
Overall width: 1680mm (66.1in)
Overall height: 1224mm (48.2in)
Unladen weight: 1105kg (2,238lb)

Performance

Top speed: 195km/h (121mph)
0-62mph: 9.7 seconds

Layout and chassis

Two-seat open-top sports car, steel monocoque, steel and plastic panels

Engine

Type: Mazda, four-cylinder inline
Block material: Cast iron
Head material: Aluminium
Cooling: Water
Bore and stroke: 83 x 85mm
Capacity: 1840 cc
Valves: Four valves per cylinder, 16 in total, DOHC
Compression ratio: 9.5:1
Carburation: Multi-port electronic fuel injection
Maximum power (DIN): 138bhp at 7,000rpm
Maximum torque: 161Nm (119lb ft) at 4,500rpm
Fuel capacity: 50ltr (11Imp gal)

Transmission

Gearbox: Mazda 5-speed manual, all synchromesh (6-speed manual optional)
Clutch: Single dry plate
Ratios　1st 3.136:1 (3.760:1)
　　　　2nd 1.888:1 (2.269:1)
　　　　3rd 1.330:1 (1.646:1)
　　　　4th 1.000:1 (1.257:1)
　　　　5th 0.814:1 (1.000:1)
　　　　6th 0.843:1 (optional)
　　　　Reverse 3.758:1
Final drive 4.100:1 (3.909:1)

Suspension and Steering

Front: Independent double wishbones, gas-filled dampers
Rear: Independent double wishbones, gas-filled dampers
Steering: Rack and pinion, hydraulic power assistance
Tyres: 195/50 R15
Wheels: Aluminium alloy, 15in
Rim width: 6in

Brakes

Type: Ventilated discs front, solid discs rear
Size: 254mm (10in) front, 251mm (9.9in) rear

Dimensions

Track
Front: 1415mm (55.7in)
Rear: 1440mm (56.7in)
Wheelbase: 2266mm (89.2in)
Overall length: 3975mm (156.5in)
Overall width: 1680mm (66.1in)
Overall height: 1224mm (48.2in)
Unladen weight: 1025kg (2,260lb)

Performance

Top speed: 197km/h (122mph)
0-62mph: 8.5 seconds

Key Rival: MGF (1995-2002) and MGTF (2002-2005 and 2007-2011)

When the original MX-5 was unveiled, MG was still selling a sports car of its own – the V8-engined RV8. It didn't take long for MG to decide to build a real competitor though, and the MGF was the product that ensued.

It was an instant success. Like the Mazda, it used humble mechanicals – Metro subframes and a standard K-Series engine, for example – and for many years even knocked the MX-5 off its perch as the UK's best-selling sports car. For a time it rivalled the MX-5, but like many other MG Rover products it eventually grew well past its sell-by date. Even so, the MGF was a car for Britain to be proud of – just like its historical forebears.

MG then released the updated TF in 2002. Ditching the Hydragas suspension of the F, its handling was improved and some road tests even rated it higher than the Mazda, but soon after, MG Rover folded. While production was started under new Chinese ownership a few years later, the car was by now hugely outdated.

Milestone – MX-5 number 531,890

The celebration of 531,890 cars built might seem like an arbitrary number to the casual observer. For Mazda, however, it is very significant. The number marks the milestone at which, in May 2000, the MX-5 became the biggest selling two-seat, open-top roadster ever.

Mazda officially applied for certification in November 1999, as production passed the half-million mark. By May the following year, Guinness World Records had officially recognised the current total, a number that continued to rise as Mazda celebrated its milestone – passing 565,779 units by the end of June 2000. The company has subsequently commemorated several other production milestones as the sales keep rising.

Comments were mixed regarding the new car's rear-end treatment, with the third brake light taking some flak. Though appreciated as an extra safety measure, some reviewers felt its place on the re-profiled boot lid spoiled the lines of the back end. Opinions on the interior were also mixed. It was certainly a more comfortable, welcoming environment than the slightly sparse Mk1 MX-5 provided, but several of the small detail changes were criticised. Chief among these was the ungainly digital clock in the middle of the dashboard, which would have been unbecoming on a budget stereo system, let alone a sports car. Unsurprisingly, this was a feature that disappeared when the MX-5 was revised a few years later.

The italicised dials were not as popular as the clear originals, and felt a little less special without the chrome-ringed accents. Many also found the large four-spoke airbag steering wheels in all but the 1.8iS models to be somewhat ugly – though their contribution to safety could not be understated. The glass rear screen was welcome to all those who had experienced the ever foggy plastic screens of early models, but otherwise the roof was as easy to use and as weathertight as before, Mazda resisting

the temptation to fit an electric hood, as featured on some MX-5 rivals.

Opinion was divided over the new seats. Covered in a more tactile material than the old cloth-trimmed chairs, some felt they were now mounted too high, particularly if leather trim – which featured firmer seat padding – was chosen. It was now even more difficult for taller drivers to get comfortable, again failing to address one of the few criticisms of the original car.

Nevertheless, the MX-5 still gave keen drivers much to smile about, whether it was uncomfortable or not. Performance had not moved on to any great degree over that of the older MX-5s, owing to a little extra weight spread about the car. The 1.6 was certainly slower than the first-generation cars, though mercifully offered greater performance than the de-tuned 90bhp models of the previous few years.

Predictably, the 1.8 model was granted the most column inches, and testers praised all the qualities they had enjoyed on the previous car – sharp steering, just enough grip, throttle-adjustable balance and, overall, a sense of fun. Many also remarked that the chassis felt stiffer than on the old models thanks to Mazda's extra bracing work, though some commented that even with the extra power of the 1.8-litre engine, the handling was no longer as 'playful' as once it had been. This was no doubt in response to customer feedback; owners often bought the cars for their style, rather than their power-oversteer capabilities, but for road testers it meant just a little less fun.

The Mk2.5 MX-5 facelift modernised the styling and brought a raft of new special editions to the market. MAZDA

MAZDA MX-5 MK2.5

As with the first-generation MX-5, Mazda refused to rest on its laurels and in 2001, extensive revisions were introduced to carry the car through its next few years. With altered styling, improved engine technology and new interior fittings, the MX-5 community saw fit to christen the facelifted Mk2 with a new designation and it is now colloquially known as the Mk2.5.

Changes to the car's exterior were most obvious. At the front, new, larger and more modern light clusters replaced those of the previous car, cutting further into the front bumper and lending the front end a more aggressive, angular look. The bumper had also changed, now jutting

deeper towards the road and for the first time incorporating recesses for integrated front fog lights.

The rear end changes were more subtle, with the amber indicator lenses of old making way for fashionable clear lenses. This detail change modernised the appearance significantly. Where 15in wheels had previously been the order of the day, Mazda now offered a selection of larger 16in wheels.

The interior was also slightly updated. Gone was the oft-criticised and cheap-looking LCD clock above the single-DIN stereo, as the centre console gained a subtle redesign. The instrument cluster now featured white dials with red numbers, and the seats were re-profiled with extra side support.

All round double-wishbone suspension kept all four wheels in contact with the ground, for that true sports car feel. MAZDA

Under the bonnet, the 1.8-litre engine gained more sophisticated sequential valve timing. Simpler than some competitors' systems, which vary both intake and exhaust valve timing and lift, the system continually retards or advances the intake camshaft timing. This can be used to boost low-speed torque and high-speed power. Combined with an updated exhaust system, the engine offered a little more power than before – 144hp at 7,000rpm and 168Nm (124lb ft) of torque at 5,000rpm, 6Nm (4.4lb ft) up on the previous 1.8. Top speed had risen to 208km/h (129mph).

Mazda further improved safety on Mk2.5 models, with the anti-lock brakes now also incorporating electronic brake force distribution. This adjusts braking force depending on the grip of the surface below, helping keep the car stable even if the braking surface has varying levels of friction. Combined with driver and passenger airbags, and an improved body structure, the MX-5 achieved a four-star rating (out of a possible five) in the Euro New Car Assessment Programme (NCAP) crash tests.

Mazda updated the car again in 2004, the 15th anniversary of the MX-5 in Europe. The changes this time were focused on the interior. Once again, the basic architecture remained largely the same, but a centre console redesign brought the controls up to date. MX-5s now came with a double-DIN stereo unit with larger, easier-to-use buttons. Another change, echoed throughout the interior, was the use of brighter and more expensive-looking materials. Most new MX-5s featured a metallic finish to the centre console, air vent rings and instrument surround, and brighter white dials replaced the black instruments.

A range of options allowed customers to brighten their car's interior further, with everything from a 'roll hoop-style bar' to aluminium-finish gear knobs, handbrake grips and pedals, all available as dealer accessories. The car's standard 16in wheels were redesigned, while a new sport model offered a six-speed manual transmission, greater body structure stiffening, upgraded sports suspension with Bilstein dampers and high-performance tyres.

Some drive, others fly – but the MX-5 roadster coupé can be used in all weathers. ANTONY INGRAM

This Mk2 MX-5 has escaped the dreaded rust. ANTONY INGRAM

Technical Specifications

Mazda MX-5 1.6i (2004–2006)

Layout and chassis
Two-seat open-top sports car, steel monocoque, steel and plastic panels

Engine
Type: Mazda, four-cylinder inline
Block material: Cast iron
Head material: Aluminium
Cooling: Water
Bore and stroke: 78 x 83.6mm
Capacity: 1597 cc
Valves: Four valves per cylinder, 16 in total, DOHC
Compression ratio: 9.4:1
Carburation: Multi-port electronic fuel injection
Maximum power (DIN): 108bhp at 6,500rpm
Maximum torque: 134Nm (99lb ft) 5,000rpm
Fuel capacity: 50ltr (11Imp gal)

Transmission
Gearbox: Mazda 5-speed manual, all synchromesh
Clutch: Single dry plate
Ratios   1st 3.136:1
         2nd 1.888:1
         3rd 1.330:1
         4th 1.000:1
         5th 0.814:1
         Reverse 3.758:1
Final drive 4.300:1

Suspension and Steering
Front: Independent double wishbones, gas-filled dampers
Rear: Independent double wishbones, gas-filled dampers
Steering: Rack and pinion, hydraulic power assistance
Tyres: 185/60 R14 (195/50 R15 optional)
Wheels: Aluminium alloy, 14in (aluminium alloy, 15in optional)
Rim width: 5.5in (6in optional)

Brakes
Type: Ventilated discs front, solid discs rear
Size: 234mm (9.2in) front, 231mm (9.1in) rear

Dimensions
Track
Front: 1405mm (55.3in)
Rear: 1430mm (56.3in)
Wheelbase: 2266mm (89.2in)
Overall length: 3975mm (156.5in)
Overall width: 1680mm (66.1in)
Overall height: 1224mm (48.2in)
Unladen weight: 1105kg (2,238lb)

Performance
Top speed: 191km/h (118mph)
0–62mph: 9.7 seconds

Mazda MX-5 1.8i (2004–2006)
[figures in brackets apply to 6-speed gearbox]

Layout and chassis
Two-seat open-top sports car, steel monocoque, steel and plastic panels

Engine
Type: Mazda, four-cylinder inline
Block material: Cast iron
Head material: Aluminium
Cooling: Water
Bore and stroke: 83 x 85mm
Capacity: 1840cc
Valves: Four valves per cylinder, 16 in total, DOHC
Compression ratio: 10:1
Carburation: Multi-port electronic fuel injection
Maximum power (DIN): 144bhp at 7,000rpm
Maximum torque: 168Nm (124lb ft) at 5,000rpm
Fuel capacity: 50ltr (11Imp gal)

Transmission
Gearbox: Mazda 5-speed manual, all synchromesh (6-speed manual, all synchromesh optional)
Clutch: Single dry plate
Ratios   1st 3.136:1 [3.760:1]
         2nd 1.888:1 [2.269:1]
         3rd 1.330:1 [1.646:1]
         4th 1.000:1 [1.257:1]
         5th 0.814:1 [1.000:1]
6th 0.843:1 (optional)
         Reverse 3.758:1
Final drive 4.100:1 [3.636:1]

Suspension and Steering
Front: Independent double wishbones, gas-filled dampers
Rear: Independent double wishbones, gas-filled dampers
Steering: Rack and pinion, hydraulic power assistance
Tyres: 195/50 R15 (205/45 R16 optional)
Wheels: Aluminium alloy, 15in (16in optional)
Rim width: 6in

Brakes
Type: Ventilated discs front, solid discs rear
Size: 254mm (10in) front, 251mm (9.9in) rear

Dimensions
Track
Front: 1405mm (55.3in)
Rear: 1430mm (56.3in)
Wheelbase: 2266mm (89.2in)
Overall length: 3975mm (156.5in)
Overall width: 1680mm (66.1in)
Overall height: 1224mm (48.2in)
Unladen weight: 1065kg (2,348lb) [1100kg; 2,425lb]

Performance
Top speed: 127mph (205km/h) [129mph; 208km/h]
0–62mph: 8.5 seconds [8.4 seconds]

CHAPTER 6

DRIVING A MK2 MX-5 TODAY

To the seasoned Mk1 owner, little of the Mk2 will come as a shock, given their similarities under the skin. As objects to behold the cars display some distinct differences, but once ensconced behind the wheel, the experiences of piloting a Mk1 will quickly come flooding back.

For those not already used to the earlier MX-5, the Mk2 is a good place to start. It offers the right combination of daily comfort and fun characteristics to suit a wide audience – it's more refined than the Mk1 and more accessible than the Mk3.

The differences between the Mk1 and Mk2 are subtle. The interior changes make the Mk2 driving environment feel a little more modern and less exposed, despite the dimensions being fairly similar. The rounded dashboard, door cards and centre console feel more yielding than the square-edged trims of the Mk1, and the addition of an airbag steering wheel offers a greater impression of safety.

It is still a sporting environment however. Drivers sit lower than they would in a regular car, even if some have criticised the driving position for being a little high. This 'high' position is partly a result of the seats being redesigned to provide a little more comfort and for those who fit, the driving position is snug and supportive. The bonnet is still clearly in view which, when you're out on the road, lets you place the car with great accuracy and makes town work easier than it might otherwise be. The centre console, complete with offset handbrake and stubby gear lever like the original, is just the right height to rest an arm on – and that gear lever is within perfect reach.

The dials are large and clear, though not as classical in appearance as their simpler equivalents in the Mk1 – you are more likely to find italic script and coloured dial faces here. The central dashboard vents are now integrated into the flowing forms of the upper dash, and with only a hazard warning switch between them – there is no need for the Mk1's pop-up light switch.

Mk2 MX-5s provide a lively drive. MAZDA

Owner's view: Caroline, Wales
Mk2, 1.8 in Emerald Mica

MX-5s can occasionally become part of the family, and Caroline's green Mk2, known as Max, is definitely one of those examples. 'I wanted an MX-5 because they're pretty and I was jealous of other people having them,' she explains. 'I used to have a 1-litre hatchback, so moving straight from that to a 1.8 MX-5 was a bit of a jump – but I love the ability to overtake and not slow down on hills, or hold everyone up!' Caroline has owned the car since 2010, and it doesn't look likely to let go any time soon. 'In rainy Wales with a 100-mile (161km) round trip to work, perhaps Max is not the most sensible of cars… but I don't care.'

Space for an engine, two passengers and luggage; what more does one need? MAZDA

The quality of what one finds below the vents will depend on the age of the Mk2 being driven – early cars had a cheap appearance and that out-of-place LCD clock, while later cars were often granted shiny silver trim and a more integrated look. Both appear dated and lacking in quality now, particularly if you've experienced the more modern interior of the Mk3. Both can also be improved by choosing one of the many special edition models made throughout the car's lifespan. With numerous upgrades and unique accessories, they can turn the sporting environment of the MX-5's cockpit into something quite special. The feel of the car can vary enormously between the standard black, cloth trimmed interior and the bright, luxurious interior of an Indiana or Arctic edition, for example. And just like with its Mk1 special edition predecessor, these MX-5s can be sought after as a result.

As in the Mk1, the steering wheel and pedals are well placed for comfort and control, and even longer journeys can be comfortable. The more refined driving environment hints of the slightly softer driving experience to come. With several years of development behind it, the twin-cam, four-cylinder 1.8-litre engine is now smoother than that found in earlier cars, with vibration reduced as a result. Some of the raw, metallic edge of the first 1.6-engined cars has been lost, but next to later Mk3 cars, it is clear that much of the character has been retained. The engine is still eager to respond to the smallest of throttle inputs and the pedals feel ideally weighted, even before you've moved off. The gearshift, too, has all the precision

you would expect and is not dulled by the inclusion of a sixth gear on some models.

The extra refinement has other benefits, of course. Changes to the engines and gearing have turned the MX-5 into a more adept long-distance cruiser, not just by reducing noise and vibration, but also by improving economy. Officially, the Mk2 1.6 achieved 34.9mpg (8.1ltr/100km) at 70mph (113km/h) and the 1.8 just a little less at 33.2mpg (8.5ltr/100km).

Later Mk2.5 models with the 1.6 engine officially managed 36.2mpg (7.8ltr/100km) combined. The 1.8-engined cars with the five and six-speed manual transmissions achieved 32.5mpg (8.7ltr/100km) and 31.7mpg (8.9ltr/100km), respectively, in mixed driving, although almost 40mpg (7.1ltr/100km) was possible on a run.

Performance feels a little more potent than that of the early 1.6 models, being similar to that of the later 1.8 Mk1s. The extra torque and, in some cars, extra gear, are both as useful when cruising on the motorway as they are when tackling country roads, but even the basic 1.6, with 108hp, is surprisingly adept at both disciplines. Mk2 1.6 drivers will no doubt agree with contemporary road tests that praised

2004 Mazda MX-5 RS Coupé

Back in 1996, Mazda North America took it upon itself to preview a new kind of MX-5, eschewing the open-air roadster body for a closed-roof coupé. Painted in yellow and known as the M-Coupé, the Mk1-based car was a subtle development based on the widely available fibreglass hard top, but seamlessly incorporated into the body. The rear window was more rakish than that of the hard top accessory, now ending where the untouched boot started. The conversion also granted the driver a little more rearward visibility than a hard top owner would normally have, with a greater curve to the rear screen and two small windows behind the untouched driver and passenger side windows.

Some subtle side body mouldings and the addition of a front and rear lower spoilers completed the look, which had turned the pretty roadster into an equally pretty fixed-roof coupé. The effect was similar to that exacted on the Lotus Elan 2+2, though Mazda's placement of the fuel tank kept the M-Coupé a strict two-seater.

Unfortunately for motor show goers that year, Mazda never followed through with a production coupé based on the Mk1 MX-5. It would be another seven years before the company previewed another fixed-roof MX-5, this time based on the Mk2.5, at the 2003 Tokyo Motor Show.

This version, known as the Trial Sports, or TS, was very different to Mazda North America's concept. The fixed roof now looked a much more integral part of the shell, with a flatter rear screen and a shallower rake towards the back of the car. The boot had been re-designed too, and set at a greater angle than that found in the regular roadster. The surrounding bodywork had also been raised to meet the new roof and rather than the token pieces of glass found behind the doors in the M-Coupé, more substantial rear windows had been fitted.

While the rest of the rear metalwork remained largely unchanged compared to the Mk2.5, the front had taken on an entirely new appearance. The regular headlights and front bumper had been ditched in favour of a rounded Italian-style front end that now housed two upright, round lights, behind Perspex covers. The new front end and taller headlights had necessitated entirely new front wings, which now sat proud of the bonnet as they might on an old Ferrari or Porsche 911. The bonnet too had been re-designed, curving half way over those raised wings.

To continue the classic look, the door mirrors were replaced with smaller, round wing-mirrors and the doors gained large, white decals ready for race numerals. Changes at the back had been less dramatic. Most obvious at a glance were the new rear light fittings, which replaced each single-piece unit with two retro-style round lights. The standard rear bumper was fitted with a deeper lip, and a matte grey exhaust tip sprouted from the centre of the car, below the bumper. Completing the rear-end treatment, a ducktail spoiler and green and white TS graphics adorned the boot, a colour scheme echoed on the right front wing. Inside, the car had been fitted with two retro-style bucket seats and a full roll cage.

Like the M-Coupé, the TS was simply a design concept, inspired by old Italian sports cars like the Fiat-engined Abarths of the 1960s. It was never designed to hit the road but, unlike Mazda North America's effort, Mazda saw fit to produce a limited run of hard-roof MX-5s for the Japanese market, the model being known as the RS Coupé.

They were released in 2004, in a limited run of 350 units. The hard top added only 10kg (22lb) to the MX-5's weight, but contributed significantly to the shell's stiffness, banishing the scuttle shake familiar to MX-5 owners all over the world. Three levels of trim were available on the Coupé, trim, a sportier Type S, and a luxury-orientated Type E. In addition, the coupé could be bought with either of the contemporary engines, both with a six-speed manual gearbox.

The Mazda RS Coupé previewed a later small production run of genuine hardtop MX-5s. MAZDA

Some of the bodywork additions were a little tasteless, but Coupé Mk2s are among the most rare MX-5s. MAZDA

The RS Coupé's sleek roofline was well integrated with its body, aided by a higher boot lid and rear wings. MAZDA

Some say that Mk2 MX-5s are softer than the Mk1s, but there is still fun to be had in the corners. HAYMARKET MEDIA GROUP

Of course, Mk2 MX-5s are equally suitable for those who just want to be seen! MAZDA

the car's terrific handling and great steering. The more pliant ride quality of the later car also makes it even better than the Mk1 when the road surface becomes broken and pitted, a common scenario on British country roads.

The car has a very natural handling balance that allows even less experienced drivers to exploit the chassis, without fearing for their lives. All Mk2s are a little more neutral than their predecessors, so that any slide from the rear end is usually of the driver's own doing, rather than the unexpected result of some over-eager driving. On dry roads both cars grip well and only heavy-handed use of the throttle will provoke the back end on the 1.8; on wet roads both can be coaxed into oversteer, but neither car is snappy and unpredictable.

For most drivers, most of the time, the Mk2 might even be a better vehicle to drive than the Mk1. Those talents are even more noticeable in day-to-day driving. A driver new to MX-5s will be amazed by how docile the car can be whether driving around town, or sitting at 70mph on the motorway. The MX-5 Mk2 is a car of simple qualities – light and accurate steering, ideally-weighted pedals, and a direct gearshift. In many respects, a Mk2 can be more pleasant to drive at low speeds than many contemporary hatchbacks, if only because every input you make into one of the controls has a linear, expected output. Qualities that make the car as much fun as it is when pressing on, also improve the everyday experience just a little bit more.

The refinement, usability and economy gives drivers even fewer second thoughts about using the car everyday and in all weathers than the first-generation cars do. Many Mk1 cars, now sliding into classic territory, are reserved for sunny days and weekends. Mk1 MX-5s might attract the most partisan supporters, but ask any Mk2 driver and they'll tell you the same thing – it's still a lot of fun, but it's also the easier car to live with every day.

Milestone – MX-5 number 700,000

Ever since breaking a Guinness World Record in May 2000 as the world's top selling two-seater roadster, the MX-5 has continued to break its own record. Another significant mark passed on 5 March 2004, as the 700,000th car rolled off the Ujina production line, near Mazda HQ in Hiroshima.

The Velocity Red Mica Mazdaspeed Miata was destined for the US market, as a top-of-the-range car with its turbocharged, 1.8-litre engine. At 178hp the Mazdaspeed is among the more powerful production MX-5s. For one car on US roads however, its production number is much more significant than its engine output.

The 700,000th MX-5. MAZDA

CHAPTER 7

MAZDA MX-5 MK3 (NC)

The MX-5 Mk2 of 1998 had essentially been a thorough update of the much loved original car, with largely superficial improvements aimed at keeping the car competitive. By the mid-2000s, Mazda's direct competitors were becoming fewer and further between, but the market as a whole was developing rapidly and customers were becoming more demanding than ever before. Technology was playing an ever-increasing part in buyers' decisions and even basic city cars were taking on higher levels of equipment. Quality had also taken a step up and buyers were beginning to cast a harsh eye over the dark, cheap-feeling plastics that had been a staple of the MX-5 cabin.

It was clear that the MX-5 needed to move with the times, but replacing such a revered vehicle is no easy task. As with the Mk1, the design proposals for the next generation MX-5 were disparate. The car's popularity in markets with very different automotive ideals – markets as diverse as North America, Japan, and Europe, for example – meant that several designs were suggested.

Project planning for the model lasted quite some time, while the assembled design teams debated which direction to take. Some even suggested that the car's iconic and

In blue and without a front number plate, the Mk3's similarity to the Ibuki Concept was clear to see. MAZDA

These development sketches show a car already well on its way to becoming the next MX-5. MAZDA

The exaggerated lines of the Mk3, or NC MX-5s look as good on paper as they do on the road. MAZDA

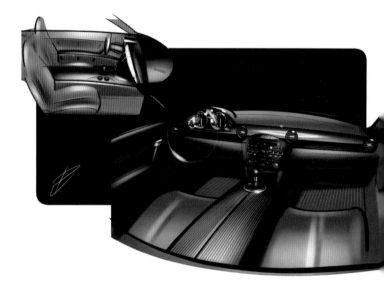

It is easy to see how the Mk3 has retained the traditional MX-5 shape. MAZDA

These sketches show how simple the basic shape of the NC's interior really is. MAZDA

traditional design language should make way for something completely different. Peter Birtwhistle, Chief Designer at Mazda Europe, recalls some of the early prototypes. 'My design team at Oberursel had four models to introduce. They were hardly recognisable as the MX-5. After a lot of customer clinics, the decision was finally made – optically, fans of the car wanted to see as few changes as possible.'

An American team put forward a concept with more grown-up appeal, less effeminate than earlier cars and more suited to a country known for its love of muscle cars. A Japanese team went for a design aimed at Japan's increasingly car-apathetic youth. Birtwhistle described the Japanese ideas as giving the impression that you could almost build the car yourself, to provide a closer, more personal relationship with it.

Mazda's 2003 Ibuki concept gave the first impressions of the next MX-5's true styling direction. Clean, compact and with a nod to the first-generation car, its dramatic wheel arches and crisp lines were clearly of the modern era, while the small headlights and rounded front grille were clear links to the original. Led by design director Moray Callum – previously at Ford and brother to Jaguar and Aston Martin designer Ian Callum – Mazda's design team gradually perfected the car's look, staying true to the MX-5's roots, while allowing engineers to make more dramatic changes under the skin.

The eventual design was a combination of the European and Japanese design studios' concepts; the interior used on the production car also originated from the European studio. Once the design had been finalised, development could get underway, led by a Japanese team including Chief Designer Yasushi Nakamuta, and Head Engineer, Takao Kijima.

A compact footprint was essential to maintaining the proportions and usable size of the previous generations. Mazda was also keen to improve passenger space, so an overall length 65mm (2.6in) greater than that of the Mk2, plus 20mm (0.8in) in extra height and an increase in width of 40mm (1.6in) facilitated extra interior space. The wheelbase had also grown, by 65mm, while the front and rear track widths benefitted from the extra body width,

ABOVE AND OPPOSITE: *The Mk3 MX-5 seems to look better with age; its similarity to the Mk1 is clear to see.* KURT ERNST

Nobuhiro Yamamoto – MX-5 Programme Manager

'I hope that the MX-5 will, in one form or another, stay around for as long as cars exist in this world.'

Yamamoto-san has been with Mazda since 1973, when he was part of the original team working on Mazda's rotary development and motor sports programme. Since then, he has become involved in programme management, a role in which he oversaw development of the RX-7, Millenia, Tribute SUV and second-generation MX-5.

In 2002, Yamamoto-san became Deputy Programme Manager for the second-generation MX-5, and since 2007 he has been Programme Manager for Mazda sports cars and he has played a significant role in MX-5 development ever since. Particularly proud of the MX-5's 2005-2006 Japan Car of the Year award, Yamamoto-san describes development of the third-generation model as his strongest memory of working at Mazda – particularly given the development team's desire to bring the prize

home to Mazda for the first time in twenty-three years.

While admitting he that he has to fill the big shoes left by previous MX-5 programme managers Toshihiko Hirai and Takao Kijima, Yamamoto-san believes he can achieve his own unique accomplishments. 'I believe that we need to further refine the essential appeal of the MX-5,' he said in 2011, 'my duty is to determine exactly what people desire… identifying what needs to be changed and what needs to stay the same.'

Speaking on the MX-5's 900,000-unit milestone in 2011, Yamamoto shared his appreciation for the hundreds of thousands of individuals who helped Mazda reach that target. 'I would like to say to owners that I hope you keep on driving, and keep on enjoying your roadster.'

With Yamamoto-san's commitment to developing the MX-5 in the future, there's every chance that hundreds of thousands more owners will keep enjoying their roadsters.

Mazda took inspiration for the Mk3 MX-5's interior from the RX-8 sports coupé. ANTONY INGRAM

increasing by 75mm (3in) at the front and 55mm (2.2in) at the rear. Impressively, the new car was only 20mm longer than the original – a far cry from the size increases typical of modern vehicles.

The designers found an extra 70mm (2.8in) of shoulder room in the cabin, and 50mm (2in) extra width at hip height. Taller drivers were also better accommodated, with seats that slid 50mm further rearwards. A new cabin design, inspired by that of Mazda's RX-8 rotary sports car, brought the interior up to date in terms of materials and quality, with textured and gloss finishes and a more ergonomic layout. At the same time, the overall feel was similar to earlier MX-5s.

A high centre console maintained the proper sports car feel and positioned the short-throw gear lever in just the right place. The car's chrome-ringed dials harked back to the original, as did the small binnacle in which they sat. And even from the new, lower, driving position, the long bonnet could still be seen through the windscreen. Mazda also improved the soft-top mechanism, which was still capable of keeping out the water, but now much easier to operate. A single, central latch, which was easier to use, replaced the two roof latches of previous MX-5s.

Easier still was the roof of one of the most significant introductions to the Mazda MX-5 stable so far – a retractable hard top roof, replacing the old soft top and accessory hard tops. Known as the Roadster Coupé (RC) in Europe and the PRHT, or 'Power Retractable Hard Top' in North America, Mazda introduced the new model in 2006. It featured a two-piece, folding plastic hardtop, operated by a switch on the dashboard. In only twelve seconds, the top could fold away into a space little bigger than that occupied by the regular soft top and required no reorganisation of the boot space to do so. Better still, RC models were barely distinguishable from their soft-topped counterparts, thanks to subtle alterations to the boot lid and more prominent rear wheel arches. Top down, the RC looked little different to the convertible, but top up the car looked modern and sophisticated, with all the benefits of refinement and security that a hard-top offers over a canvas roof.

Under that bonnet, the car's extra length now allowed for the MX-5's two new engines, both Mazda MZR four-cylinder petrols. Like the original B-series engines, the MZR range of engines is renowned for strength and durability, and has seen service in several other cars in the Mazda range. The engines are offered in 1.8 and 2.0-litre capacities, the smaller unit using a five-speed manual gearbox and the larger a six-speed manual. With 124hp, the 1.8-litre serves as the entry-level model, while an output of 158bhp made the 2.0-litre model the most powerful naturally aspirated MX-5 so far. Throttle response was still more a priority

The Mazda-developed MZR engine is sweet spinning and reliable, in keeping with the older MX-5 engines. ANTONY INGRAM

than outright horsepower, however, and back in 2005, Chief Engineer Joe Bakaj told *Autocar*, 'We measure instantaneous acceleration carefully, because that's a vital component in a sports car's performance feel'.

Construction similarities with the rotary-powered RX-8 meant that the engines could be mounted 135mm (5.3in) further back in the chassis compared to previous MX-5s, allowing engineers to maintain the car's ideal 50:50 weight distribution between the front and rear axles. Other measures to improve weight distribution included a new alloy boot lid, repositioning the fuel tank further forwards and tilting the radiator backwards to move more of its mass towards the centre of the car.

Those similarities with the RX-8 were deliberate, allowing Mazda to use a more sophisticated chassis setup than was possible with the original car. Independent double-wishbone suspension was again employed at the front end, this time shared with the RX-8, while that car also donated its five-link setup at the rear, replacing the previous double-wishbone arrangement. The changes were not made just to maintain the old car's excellent handling, but with greater suspension travel now possible, Mazda could ensure the Mk3 also featured a more forgiving ride quality – despite the larger wheel arches now comfortably accommodating 17in wheels. Advances in production techniques and the use of steel granted the car a stiffer

Milestone – MX-5 number 800,000

Mazda celebrated the production of MX-5 number 800,000 on 30 January 2007. The red soft-top roadster destined for the US market rolled off the production line seventeen years and nine months after production began in April 1989 and just a year and five months after the third-generation MX-5 had gone on sale.

The 800,000th MX-5. MAZDA

On the outside the Mk3 was very much an MX-5, but under the skin it was more advanced than ever. MAZDA

At the rear, a new five-link suspension system, derived from the RX-8's, replaced the old double-wishbone setup. MAZDA

The MX-5 Mk3's front axle retained double wishbone suspension. MAZDA

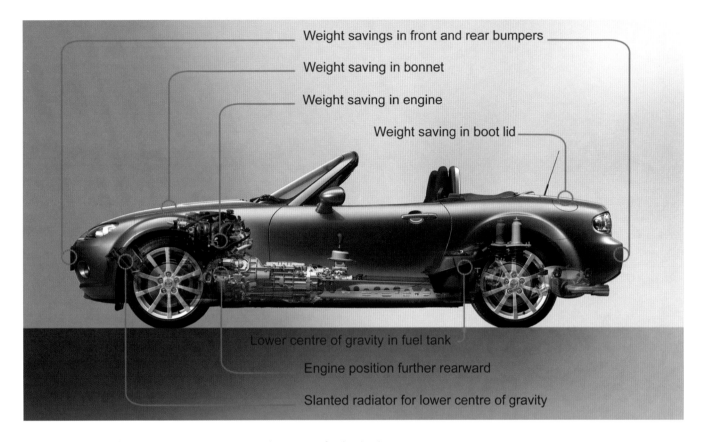

Weight savings in front and rear bumpers

Weight saving in bonnet

Weight saving in engine

Weight saving in boot lid

Lower centre of gravity in fuel tank

Engine position further rearward

Slanted radiator for lower centre of gravity

Lightweight and perfect weight distribution were two key targets for the development team. MAZDA

chassis too, helping to eliminate some of the scuttle shake found in the older cars.

Above all, Mazda had gone to great lengths to ensure that weight hardly differed from the older car, despite advances in safety, equipment and an increase in size. In promotional materials the company talked about its 'gram strategy', an engineering ethos remarkably similar to techniques used by Colin Chapman at Lotus several decades earlier – albeit with less risk to the car's users. If even a tiny amount of weight could be saved from an individual component, Mazda ensured it would be done.

The body structure actually ended up 20kg (44lb) lighter than before despite the size increase, through greater use of aluminium. Each component was weighed to ensure it did not contribute unnecessary weight to the car. One popular example, highlighted on popular TV show *Top Gear*, was that of the rear-view mirror, which was 84g (3oz) lighter than the mirror on a Mk2. Similar reductions on otherwise innocuous components resulted in a quoted kerb weight of 1127kg (2,485lb) for the 2.0-litre car – a mere 10kg (22lb) heavier than the 1.8-litre Mk2 MX-5.

These weight saving techniques were not just important for the MX-5, but were used across Mazda's range, ensuring that every succeeding model benefitted from better construction techniques and lower weight. The results in fuel efficiency, and improved handling and performance helped Mazda justify its 'Zoom-Zoom' marketing slogan.

Reception

Few cars are as eagerly awaited as a new Mazda MX-5, and much of the press was falling over itself to get drives in the latest model. The car had already seen plenty of positive reaction pre-launch. The styling, much admired on the Ibuki concept, was praised for its success in its homage to the looks of the original, while appearing suitably modern next to rivals like Honda's S2000.

However, there were still a few reservations. Some felt the styling lacked the delicacy of the older models, while others suggested that the car's ride height looked too

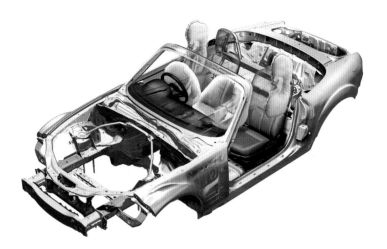
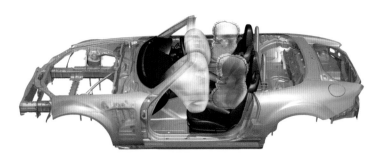

ABOVE AND RIGHT: *The Mk3's steel shell was lightweight and strong.* MAZDA

Owner's view: Kurt, Florida
Mk3, Galaxy Grey 2.0 Sport

As the previous owner of a Mk1 MX-5, Kurt broke one of his own rules – never buy the same model of car twice – when he bought a 2006 MX-5 Sport. After driving several examples of Honda's S2000 roadster, he dismissed the high-revving MX-5 rival due to its highly-strung nature, which was less fun on the daily commute than it sounded. Bought in February 2006, the Sport didn't stay standard for long. Kurt soon added Mazdaspeed springs and sway bars, a Flyin' Miata exhaust system, a Voodoo gear knob and leather gaiters for the gear and handbrake levers.

So why an MX-5? 'The handling. To this day I can jump into any Mk3 MX-5 and immediately drive it at the limit of its tyres, which is something I can't say for any other car on the market. It forgives mistakes with a slap on the wrist, not a punch to the face!' Kurt has plenty of ideas about his ideal 2.0-litre MX-5 too. 'It would make a normally aspirated 225hp and 250lb ft [339Nm] of torque, have a kerb weight of 1050kg [2,315lb] and be fitted with uprated coilover suspension. A Voodoo shift knob, which has graced my Mk1 and Mk3 MX-5s, would be an essential item.'

high. If imitation is the sincerest form of flattery, then Mazda was certainly flattering the Mk1 MX-5, also criticised on occasion for its lofty stance, but on the Mk3 it hinted at deeper rooted problems as journalists got out on the road in the new car.

Most reviews were unsurprisingly positive. The old MX-5 had remained a class-leader right up until its replacement and with greater levels of cabin quality, more space, better performance and more torsional rigidity than the Mk2, the Mk3 could do little wrong in these departments. Reviewers liked the new RX-8-inspired cabin design, the extra boot space and the mechanical refinement of the new MZR engines.

The cabin was certainly an improvement. For those who previously found the MX-5 cabin a little small, particularly taller drivers, the new lowered driving position and higher window line helped them feel more a part of the car – typically described as 'sitting in, rather than on' the seats. Comfort was improved over longer distances in the new seats, while the engines' extra refinement made holding conversations even easier than it had previously been.

However, there were dissenting voices over the car's handling. In many ways it was not dissimilar to the later Mk2 cars, but all was not well in some departments. Testers in several magazines criticised the car for lacking steering feel. Mazda had moved from hydraulic to electric assistance with the MX-5 and the technology, still in its relative infancy, had left drivers with little idea of what the front tyres were doing.

The Mk3 may be more refined, but it is still capable of raising a smile in the turns. MAZDA

This compounded the second issue, which was that many drivers felt the handling balance was a little too snappy, even when driven at moderate pace and particularly on wet roads. Many criticised the ride height and others suggested that the lack of steering feel meant that it was almost impossible to tell when the car was about to lose grip. A combination of other factors was deemed to be at fault, from an imbalance between front and rear spring and damper rates – too stiff at the front, too soft at the rear – to sloppy pre-delivery inspections, which failed to correctly set the car's geometry as Mazda intended.

Renowned enthusiast's magazine *EVO* even set up a feature to discover whether the MX-5 had really lost its magic, comparing the 1.8 and 2.0-litre Mk3 models, before com-

paring the new car to its Mk1 and Mk2 predecessors. The prognosis wasn't good. The May 2006 issue reported: 'The handling balance feels forced, unnatural… neither [1.8 nor 2.0] felt a patch on the old MX-5s of fond memory.'

Testers concluded that while the 1.8 felt better to drive than the 2.0 in Sport trim, the stability control-equipped 2.0-litre car was the wiser choice, simply to provide a safety barrier should the car catch out unwary drivers. Many reviewers also concluded that the car improved significantly on the optional £299 Mazdaspeed Eibach spring kit, which lowered it by 35mm (1.4in). This improved the handling and the car's looks, and it's no surprise that Mazda's later tweaks included lower ride height as standard.

Key Rival – Mk3 Subaru BRZ and Toyota GT 86, (2012-present)

Of all the MX-5 rivals Mazda has seen come and go over the years, the joint efforts of Subaru and Toyota on the BRZ and GT 86 are perhaps the most intriguing. More than any other cars since the original MX-5, the BRZ and '86 stand for pure, simple driving fun.

Giving their products narrow tyres, relatively low weight, a front-mounted engine, rear-drive layout and limited-slip differentials, the two companies have shunned the modern pursuit of increasing power to increase thrills, relying instead on precise controls and tactile feedback – exactly the attributes that made the MX-5 so much fun back in 1989.

Amusingly, these cars have even received the same criticisms as their spiritual predecessor, including below-par cabin materials and a lack of power. Both have already become revered, but whether they stand up to the test of time quite as well as the MX-5 remains to be seen.

Mk3 MX-5s offer all the thrills of their earlier counterparts, but with a little more refinement. MAZDA

The classic influence is apparent in early Mk3 models. MAZDA

MX-5s can be surprisingly practical, but a surfboard may be a little too much! MAZDA

The MX-5 Le Mans paint scheme replicated that of the 787B Le Mans-winning racecar. MAZDA

Technical Specifications, MX-5 Mk1

Mazda MX-5 1.8i (2007–to date)

Layout and chassis
Two-seat open-top sports car, steel monocoque, steel and plastic panels

Engine
Type: Mazda, four-cylinder inline
Block material: Aluminium
Head material: Aluminium
Cooling: Water
Bore and stroke: 83 x 83.1mm
Capacity: 1798 cc
Valves: Four valves per cylinder, 16 in total, DOHC
Compression ratio: 10.8:1
Carburation: Sequential multi-port electronic fuel injection
Maximum power (DIN): 124bhp at 6,500rpm
Maximum torque: 167Nm (123lb ft) at 4,500rpm
Fuel capacity: 50ltr (11Imp gal)

Transmission
Gearbox: Mazda 5-speed manual, all synchromesh
Clutch: Single dry plate
Ratios   1st 3.136:1
         2nd 1.888:1
         3rd 1.330:1
         4th 1.000:1
         5th 0.814:1
         Reverse 3.758:1
Final drive 4.100:1

Suspension and Steering
Front: Independent double wishbones, gas-filled dampers
Rear: Multi-link
Steering: Rack and pinion, hydraulic power assistance
Tyres: 205/50 R16 (205/45 R17 optional)
Wheels: Aluminium alloy, 16in (aluminium alloy, 17in optional)
Rim width: 6.5in (7in optional)

Brakes
Type: Ventilated discs front, solid discs rear
Size: 290mm (11.4in) front, 279mm (11in) rear

Dimensions
Track
Front: 1490mm (58.7in)
Rear: 1495mm (58.9in)
Wheelbase: 2330mm (91.7in)
Overall length: 3995mm (157.3in)
Overall width: 1720mm (67.7in)
Overall height: 1255mm (49.4in)
Unladen weight: 1075kg (2,270lb)

Performance
Top speed: 194km/h (120mph) (198km/h/121mph Roadster Coupé)
0–60mph: 9.9 seconds (to 62mph)

Mazda MX-5 2.0i (2007–to date)

Layout and chassis
Two-seat open-top sports car, steel monocoque, steel and plastic panels

Engine
Type: Mazda, four-cylinder inline
Block material: Aluminium
Head material: Aluminium
Cooling: Water
Bore and stroke: 87.5 x 83.1mm
Capacity: 1999cc
Valves: Four valves per cylinder, 16 in total, DOHC
Compression ratio: 10.8:1
Carburation: Sequential multi-port electronic fuel injection
Maximum power (DIN): 158bhp at 6,700rpm
Maximum torque: 188Nm (139lb ft) at 5,000rpm
Fuel capacity: 50ltr (11Imp gal)

Transmission
Gearbox: Mazda 6-speed manual, all synchromesh (6-speed automatic optional)
Clutch: Single dry plate
Ratios   1st 3.820:1 (3.538:1)
         2nd 2.260:1 (2.060:1)
         3rd 1.640:1 (1.404:1)
         4th 1.180:1 (1.000:1)
         5th 1.000:1 (0.713:1)
         6th 0.830:1 (0.582:1)
         Reverse 3.603:1 (3.168:1)
Final drive 4.100:1

Suspension and Steering
Front: Independent double wishbones, gas-filled dampers
Rear: Multi-link
Steering: Rack and pinion, hydraulic power assistance
Tyres: 205/50 R16 (205/45 R17 optional)
Wheels: Aluminium alloy, 16in (aluminium alloy, 17in optional)
Rim width: 6.5in (7in optional)

Brakes
Type: Ventilated discs front, solid discs rear
Size: 290mm (11.4in) front, 279mm (11in) rear

Dimensions
Track
Front: 1490mm (58.7in)
Rear: 1495mm (58.9in)
Wheelbase: 2330mm (91.7in)
Overall length: 3995mm (157.3in)
Overall width: 1720mm (67.7in)
Overall height: 1255mm (49.4in)
Unladen weight: 1090kg (2,403lb) (1100kg/2,425lb for automatic)

Performance
Top speed: 213km/h (132mph) (194km/h/120mph automatic; 218km/h/135mph Roadster Coupé)
0–62mph: 7.9 seconds (8.9 seconds automatic)

Visible here, Mazda continued with its 'Power Plant Frame' concept in Mk3 MX-5s.
MAZDA

It was not all bad news for the MX-5, however, and observing with a less critical eye, many found the car as rewarding as previous examples, but better in other tangible areas. *Autocar* took a Mk3 from the UK to Val Thorens, France, shortly after the model had been launched, along with a Ford Focus ST hot hatchback and a Porsche Cayman. Not only did the MX-5 perform well on the long motorway runs and snow-covered mountain passes, but it was also decreed the most fun.

Despite concerns over the handling of the earliest models, Mazda gradually worked away at improving the Mk3 and it is generally accepted that as an all-round vehicle, the Mk3 MX-5 is better than previous generations. Whether it is a better MX-5 is very much up to individual interpretation.

MAZDA MX-5 MK3.5

After the Mk3's sometimes frosty reception, Mazda needed to make its updates count if the Mk3.5 was to avoid similar criticism. The previous car's styling rarely came in for negative comment, but a visual refresh brought the Mk3.5 further in line with other models in the range, including the recently facelifted RX-8 sports car, and the Mazda2, Mazda3 and Mazda6 volume models. It brought marginally larger headlamps, which were now angled slightly downwards and a large central grille to replace the smaller, rounder opening of the pre-facelift model. Together with a more aggressive bumper design and larger Mazda badge on the nose, the changes endowed the Mk3.5 with a distinct 'face', which was more apparent in some colours than others.

NO AIRCRAFT
PARKING
AT ANY TIME

N333 NNU

The Roadster Coupé's hardtop has been a very popular addition to the MX-5 range.
ANTONY INGRAM

Roof down, it's difficult to tell the Roadster Coupé from a regular soft-top MX-5. ANTONY INGRAM

This Mk3.5 Roadster Coupé looks sophisticated and expensive. ANTONY INGRAM

Styling changes aft of the front end were minimal, with only the addition of jewel-like red and clear light clusters changing the appearance to any real degree. New side skirts were fitted, however, and combined with the revised front end, contributed to a slight improvement in the car's aerodynamics. Mazda continued to offer both the manual soft top and electronically retractable hard top roof options, the designs of which remained unchanged.

Inside, the dashboard design remained largely unchanged from the previous car's, but Mazda made an effort to improve some of the materials used, for greater perceived quality. In a change less easily perceived but certainly practical, Mazda also changed the door-mounted cupholders that had intruded on legroom for larger drivers in the preceding car. These were now better integrated into the door cards and remained flush with the door pulls.

The range-topping 2.0-litre engine kept the same 158hp output, but now reached this figure at 7,000rpm, rather than 6,700rpm. The engineers also worked hard to improve the car's sound, giving the engine a deeper growl while reducing unwanted noise in the cabin. Fuel economy with both five- and six-speed manual transmissions also improved, by 4 and 7 per cent, respectively. The 1.8-litre engine was paired with a revised gearbox, sporting a longer final drive ratio. This improved economy by a respectable 4 per cent, for a combined 7ltr/100km (40.3mpg).

For the first time in Europe, Mazda also offered the option of a six-speed automatic transmission on the 2.0-litre MX-5. Using a torque converter rather than the increasingly common dual-clutch automated setup, drivers could leave the gearbox in Drive as on a regular automatic, or choose to shift manually using either the central shifter, or steering wheel-mounted paddles. The shift lever used a race-style sequential action, pulling backwards to change up and pushing forwards to change down. In contrast, the wheel paddles were a little unorthodox. Rather than the typical left and right paddles for changing down or up, the MX-5 used two up-shift paddles – both mounted on the reverse of the steering wheel – and two down-shift buttons, on the upperside of both spokes on the steering wheel. The system is not dissimilar to the Tiptronic setup found in many Porsche models, though the confusing layout is reflected in Porsche's recent decision to change to something more conventional.

Continual improvement to the suspension setup had resulted in a car that now drove as 'good as it looked', and magazine road tests universally praise the car's handling. The steering was retuned for more feel, and the suspension upgraded to improve the car's balance.

The Kuro special edition stands out with its racing stripes and metallic paintwork. ANTONY INGRAM

Mk3 MX-5s look more aggressive than their predecessors. ANTONY INGRAM

Mazda is rightly proud of the MX-5 and its badge takes centre stage on the car's nose. ANTONY INGRAM

Stainless kick plates are a popular feature of special editions. ANTONY INGRAM

Specification on Mk3.5s is typically high – projector-style headlamps are standard and fog lights are a common feature. ANTONY INGRAM

Badging on the front wing identifies many of the special editions, including the Kuro.

The Mk3.5 MX-5 gained Mazda's corporate family face. ANTONY INGRAM

Milestone – MX-5 number 900,000

February 4, 2011 marked a significant milestone for the Mazda MX-5, with the construction of the 900,000th unit, twenty-one years and ten months after the very first MX-5 rolled off the line. Mazda once again applied to Guinness World Records to have the total updated, following previous milestones at 700,000 and 800,000 units, after the original record was broken in May 2000 with well over 500,000 units.

The 900,000th MX-5 was a German-market 2.0-litre soft top, in Copper Red Mica. The company used the record production number to reiterate its commitment to developing the MX-5 for the future – having successfully updated the car since its 1989 debut to keep up with changing buyer trends, environmental issues and production techniques.

MX-5 milestones.
MAZDA

CHAPTER 8

DRIVING A MK3 MX-5 TODAY

The Mk3 Mazda MX-5 is at once very familiar and very different to fans of the older machines, neatly echoing the ethos and development of the car compared to its predecessors. From the outside the car seems slightly larger, though not hugely so unless the new and old cars are parked side-by-side. In contrast to many vehicles, however, the MX-5 is still relatively small, although attractively proportioned. Its DNA is very evident, even in Mk3.5 facelift models that brought it more in line with Mazda's mainstream cars. The long bonnet is still present, as is the curved windscreen, subtle bulge in the bonnet and small,

rounded taillights. At the same time, it looks chunkier, in a way that modern cars often do, and rides on larger wheels with lower profile tyres, lending an aggression not matched by the Mk1 and Mk2.

The interior changes are noticeable when climbing from one car to the other, and although the Mk3 is itself now starting to age, it offers a more cosy and well thought-out environment than in earlier MX-5s. Importantly, the basics are still present and correct – clear instruments, a low, comfortable driving position and well-placed controls. Most drivers should be able to instantly climb in and find

The Roadster Coupé's hardtop lines barely differ from that of the soft-top, although it brings a raft of benefits.
ANTONY INGRAM

Not everyone is keen on the Mk3.5's smiley face, but it gives a clear visual link to the rest of the Mazda range. ANTONY INGRAM

At the back, inspiration from the original car is clearly be seen. ANTONY INGRAM

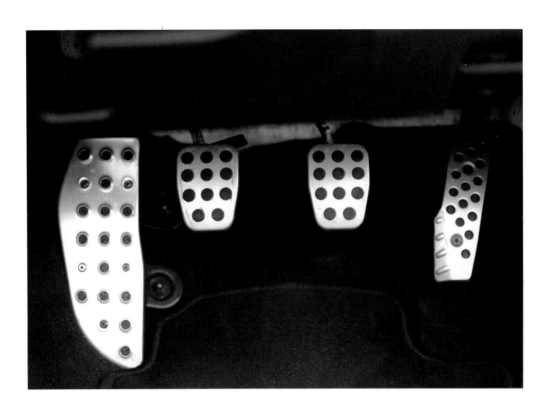

Well-spaced for sporting driving, the pedals offer great feedback.
ANTONY INGRAM

their ideal driving position and previous MX-5 owners will feel at home. Some may find there's a little less space in the footwell and that the pedals a little more offset to the right. This feels more unusual for those who've never driven a rear-drive car before – it's a result of the wide transmission tunnel required to fit the gearbox. Drivers soon get used to it.

The larger dashboard, doorcards and plastic bulkhead behind the two seats make the interior a little less airy than that of older MX-5s, and while the parcel shelf behind the seats is larger, it is no longer as accessible as it once was – though Mazda recommends against storing items there if you plan to stow the roof at any stage. The company improved the quality of the cabin materials for Mk3.5 cars, and these will also come better specified, particularly on special edition models. Many will have leather seats, for example, with leather trim on the doorcards and other areas.

The roof is as simple as ever to operate, though operation depends on whether you choose the regular, manual soft top, or the electrically operated hard roof. In the soft top, a large central handle replaces the two handles on older MX-5s. Press a button to unlock the catch, pull the handle, and the roof unlatches. The hood can then be flipped back with two handles, though thanks to the more

sophisticated mechanism, it requires a little more effort than the one-handed shove that sufficed in earlier models. The roof drops back and can be secured by clicking it into position behind you, without need of a tonneau cover.

In the Roadster Coupé, the roof is once again unlocked with a manual latch, but after that the entire operation is automatic, using a button on the centre console. Press this, and the rear deck lid rises up, before the two-piece hard top folds in on itself and disappears beneath the bulkhead. The deck lid then closes, and your open-air experience can begin. Cleverly, Mazda has ensured that boot space is unaffected by the roof and the only external giveaway that you're driving the hardtop model when the roof is closed, is a slightly higher line to the body, aft of the seats.

Though Mazda made improvements to the Mk1 and Mk2 cars throughout their life cycles, the Mk3 is still a much more refined vehicle on start up, thanks to the MZR unit that replaced the old 1.8 and 1.6 engines. It is smoother and quieter, and settles into a low, emission-friendly idle more quickly, though it lacks the rough-and-ready element of classic sports cars evoked by predecessors – an increasingly unacceptable facet in a market demanding greater refinement. There's less of a burble from the exhaust pipe, though there's still a hard, metallic

The Mk3, just like the earlier models, has a crisp gearshift. ANTONY INGRAM

edge to the sound that suggests it is a little more special than the engine's normal home in Mazda 3s and 6s. That feeling continues with a few blips of the throttle, an eager rasp suggesting the MX-5 is still very much a sports car, even if it has gained some refinements on the way.

Performance from the 2.0-litre engine is stronger than that offered by earlier MX-5s, with the benchmark 0-62mph sprint accomplished in 7.9 seconds. The 1.8-litre cars are two seconds slower over the same increment and also lack the 2.0's 130mph-plus top speed, though this is of dubious relevance in most countries. The 2.0 is said to be a better cruiser at higher speeds thanks to its extra gear, but both cars offer more than enough performance to keep up with modern traffic. Motorway cruising can be improved further by opting for the Roadster Coupé, with its folding hard top. This cuts out much of the wind roar present with the soft-top roof.

Playing with the controls does nothing to cast any doubts about the car's ethos. The gear lever is still stubby, the clutch still usefully light, and the brake pedal firmer than on most family cars. On the move, the Mk3 immediately comes alive, and anyone familiar with the older models will quickly appreciate the keenness with which it turns into corners, the fast and precise throw of the gear change and the instant throttle response. These factors

combine to make the MX-5 as fun at low speeds as the previous models, the extra refinement making it all the more liveable.

Some owners may find the automatic even easier to use, though the subject of which is the better transmission is the cause of much debate on owners' forums. It promises a sporty feel with paddle-operated gear changing, but Mazda has adopted an unusual system that owners get used to, even though most would prefer the more traditional option of right and left up- and down-change paddles. Changes can also be made using the sequential gear selector – which ironically uses a more traditional layout, pulling back to effect an up-change and forward to select a lower gear. Of course, drivers can also take the more relaxing option, leaving the car in Drive to make light work of traffic or the daily commute.

The car's usability is particularly apparent on rough roads, where although body shake has not yet been eliminated, the Mk3 is leagues ahead of the older vehicles. The extra suspension travel over previous MX-5s also allows the Mk3 to more comfortably deal with bumps and ruts in the road. With the roof on Roadster Coupé models erected, wobbles from the chassis are virtually absent thanks to the extra stiffness of the hard roof. All models feel well built too, refusing to rattle, even over fairly harsh

Peter Birtwhistle – Chief Designer
at Mazda Motor Europe since 1999

Peter Birtwhistle. MAZDA

'*Our MX-5 is an outstanding example of how simple solutions are often the best ones.*'

Starting as Senior Designer at Mazda in 1988, Birtwhistle is now Chief Designer at Mazda Motor Europe's Research & Development Centre in Oberursel, Germany.

He studied automotive design at the Royal College of Art in London, before joining design teams in several large car companies. In an interview with Mazda Australia, he revealed his influences as virtually anything mechanical – from cars, through aircraft, to boats. He also classes himself as a fan of product designer Phillipe Starck and his favourite car is the Jaguar E-Type.

Before joining Mazda, Birtwhistle had previously held positions as exterior studio chief designer at Porsche, and studio designer at Audi and Vauxhall.

Having worked at Mazda for more than twenty years, Birtwhistle has played a part in the majority of Mazda's most significant models. From the 323F 'five-door coupé' and later 323 and 626 family cars, through the luxurious Xedos range, to the first-generation Mazda6, both generations of Mazda3, the Mazda5 and several concept vehicles Peter worked on them all.

He also contributed to the third-generation MX-5 and believes that part of Mazda's design success is to do with the company's relatively small size. 'The vehicles remain the absolute focus,' he says. 'This focus is ultimately reflected in the design of Mazda vehicles.' Working on the design of the next-generation MX-5 is unlikely to be easy, but Birtwhistle wants to '…keep its character, maintain a lower weight and evolve the design language.'

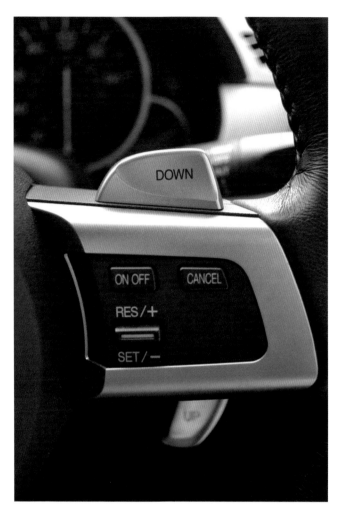

Purists prefer the manual gearbox, but the automatic could be considered vital for city drivers. ANTONY INGRAM

Paddles operate the gear changes on the auto. Pulling the back paddle changes up, push the front paddle changes down. ANTONY INGRAM

bumps in the road. Subjectively, the car also feels more solid than its predecessors, thanks to the more substantial interior fittings, chunky windscreen surround – which restricts vision a little in corners – and the relative lack of noise.

Over rough or smooth, the ride quality has improved over the older models. Where some surfaces would have the older cars bobbing, weaving and shaking, the Mk3 takes these roads in its stride. Ride quality is firm but rarely uncomfortable, and is unlikely to make you wince at every pothole and motorway expansion joint. That's all the more impressive considering the trend towards larger wheels – even 17in wheels don't seem to compromise the MX-5's flow over rougher surfaces.

Early Mk3 press reports initially questioned whether the MX-5's famed handling had fallen by the wayside, with poor steering feel and an unusually high ride height contributing to tricky handling. Mazda quickly brought about a fix, equipping 2.0-litre models with Eibach springs and Bilstein dampers to improve matters, but Mk3.5 models were even better and offer most of the fun with greater safety than before.

On 17in wheels and wide tyres the grip initially feels limitless, particularly in the dry. The car certainly doesn't roll as much as older MX-5s, which allows drivers to carry greater speed through the corners. No longer is the car as eager to break sideways under high cornering loads, a relief for anyone who was caught off-guard in the

The Mk3.5 MX-5 is more mature, but just as fun as ever. ANTONY INGRAM

older models. In the wet the car moves around much more under power, and even breaks traction a little before the standard-fit stability control and traction control rein in any slides.

Drivers with more experience will be pleased to learn that the safety systems can be disabled with a simple button press, allowing them to greater exploit the chassis. With even weight distribution, direct steering and a minimum of 126hp going to the rear wheels in the 1.8 model, it is possible to provoke lurid slides that need quick reactions to recover – many drivers would be best served by keeping the traction control engaged!

Keen drivers weaned on the original cars may also miss the extra tactility of hydraulically assisted steering. While offering good feel by modern standards, the electric assistance of the Mk3 lacks some of the feedback of the Mk1 and Mk2. The steering is not alone in diluting some of the feel, and the electric throttle and increased braking assistance also play a part. Throttle response doesn't initially feel quite as sharp as on earlier cars with cable systems and while few will complain about the short, anti-lock assisted emergency braking, some pedal feel has been lost.

Day to day though, virtually all of these changes can be considered acceptable compromises for a vehicle which is more than ever a car that can be used every day. It maintains the MX-5's age-old ability to entertain, even when not exploring its limits, which makes it a far more usable sports car than some offering greater power. Modern conveniences like a decent stereo and – on some models – air conditioning, mean it is even more suited to year-round use. Quick steering makes light work of city traffic and a responsive engine makes light work of motorway journeys. On the latter, most drivers will achieve more than 8.1ltr/100km (35mpg) – and 1.8 owners may even see 7.1ltr/100km (40mpg) at the legal limit. Long trips are not out of the question and shouldn't break the bank, which is even more important than it was back in 1989, given today's fuel prices.

Many will feel that small sacrifices in ultimate driving dynamics are an acceptable compromise for every-day usability as even the most basic cars become evermore competent. Importantly, while more comfortable, quicker, quieter, better equipped and safer than ever, the MX-5 is still as much fun as it ever was.

CHAPTER 9

PRODUCTION AND SALES

As Mazda's production counter rolls on towards one million units, there is little doubt that the MX-5 has been a sales success. In fact, from the car's first full year of production and sales, the signs were already there that Mazda had produced a car with huge commercial potential.

After an initial twelve vehicles had been produced in 1988, all pre-production cars not intended for sale, the MX-5's first full year of production was 1989. That year, 45,266 units were produced, 34,021 of which were designated for export.

Even without European sales in 1989, the combined sales from Japan, the United States, Canada and Australia totalled 35,807 units. America's contribution alone was over 23,000 sales, and the country has subsequently been by far the biggest consumer of MX-5s. By the end

A Mk1 Mazda MX-5. PETE KENT // @NOTPOSHPETE

of 2011, total cumulative sales in the US had totalled 382,758 units – over a third of all the MX-5s ever produced. By comparison, home market sales have run at around half that of what America has been buying.

Cumulative sales had already topped 100,000 units by the end of the car's first full year on sale worldwide, in 1990. By that time, production had reached over 140,000 units. Production broke 200,000 units in 1991, 300,000 by 1993, 400,000 by 1996 and the half-million mark passe–d in 1999, during the Mk2 MX-5's production run. Sales were not far behind with in excess of 236,000 MX-5s having reached customers by the end of 1992 and by 1999, cumulative sales topped 516,682 units.

To date, Mazda has not yet matched the buzz of those early years in terms of production and sales. In particular, 1990 was a highlight for the company, with sales well underway in North America and Japan, and European customers finally able to get their hands on the car. That year, Mazda manufactured 95,640 MX-5s. Sales reached their highest totals in Japan and the US, with 25,226 and 35,944 cars sold, respectively. Europe saw over 9,000 sales and Australia contributed over 1,400. By the end of the year, 75,789 MX-5s had been sold worldwide.

Debut years have since been the most successful for each generation of the MX-5, even if no subsequent car has quite generated the clamour seen in those early years. The first year of the Mk2, 1998, saw production figures of over 58,600 and sales of 49,205. America alone bought almost 20,000 cars. The Mk3's first year, 2006, was also a high-seller. American drivers bought 16,897 of the new 'MX-5 Miata', but subsequently sales have dropped and are unlikely to match those heady highs until a new model appears.

The earliest cars were clearly a highlight for Mazda and their sales reflect just how important the MX-5 has been on a global scale. Production of 900,000 units is relatively small by the standards of family cars, but for a sports car it is huge. For such a humble vehicle, the MX-5 has punched well above its weight since it debuted in 1989.

This 1.8-litre Kuro edition features red paintwork, racing stripes and dark-painted alloy wheels. ANTONY INGRAM

The badge may have changed, but the taillights hark back to earlier MX-5 models. ANTONY INGRAM

Despite appearances, it is still relatively easy to service later MX-5s at home. ANTONY INGRAM

Boot space is improved over earlier cars, but drivers still need to pack lightly. *ANTONY INGRAM*

The watertight hood is appreciated on a rainy day. *ANTONY INGRAM*

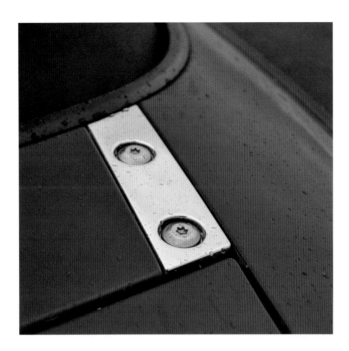

Accessory hard tops attach using so-called 'Frankenstein bolts'. *ANTONY INGRAM*

The MX-5's dials are easy to read. *ANTONY INGRAM*

Usefully, the Mk3 features special air vent settings for when the roof is lowered. *ANTONY INGRAM*

Light, sleek and a lot of fun – and the aircraft aren't bad either! ANTONY INGRAM

This grey Mk3.5 features a 2.0-litre engine and Sport trim. ANTONY INGRAM

CHAPTER 10

LIMITED EDITIONS

Since the Mk1 MX-5 originally went on sale, a bewildering number of limited edition models has been released. While some exist solely to offer a particular colour scheme or trim level, others have been responsible for introducing new mechanical elements to the range. Some, including the Anniversary models, have developed a popular following.

The following list will be particularly useful for potential MX-5 buyers, since it's easy to become overwhelmed by the number of special editions that appear in classified adverts and on internet auction sites. It will also allow a double-check for the correct specification – many cars have been modified, upgraded or repaired and some may have lost the unique features that define them. Some alloy wheel designs and decals are particularly difficult to get hold of, so it's

always worth ensuring that the model you are considering has all the attributes it left the factory with.

The next few pages will also introduce many of the unique models available in the UK and Japan, some of which are particularly rare and very highly specified. These are particularly sought after by enthusiasts and may command surprisingly high prices on the rare occasions they come up for sale.

1989 – V-SPECIAL (JAPAN)

The Eunos Roadster V-Special, or V-Spec as it is often known in MX-5 circles, is one of the more recognisable and desirable versions of the MX-5 once sold in Mazda's home market. While every inch the sports car, the emphasis was on

The Eunos V-Spec Roadster is one of the most sought after MX-5s.
ANTONY INGRAM

British Racing Green paint and a tan hood bring back memories of old British sports cars. ANTONY INGRAM

The V-Spec has a luxurious interior, topped by a beautiful Nardi wooden steering wheel. ANTONY INGRAM

The V-Spec is one of the most sought after MX-5s. MAZDA

traditional luxury and several unique features transform the car from a quite spartan vehicle into something much more upmarket, with the retro factor also moved up a notch. The latter begins with the paintwork, in traditional British Racing Green – officially known as Neo Green– which gives the car even more of an illusion of old British sports cars.

The V-Spec was supplied as standard with the 14in Enkei 'daisies' of the regular Eunos and MX-5, but an optional multi-spoke BBS design was also available, adding just a touch more class to the car's exterior. That class was most evident on the inside, however, with the cabin dominated by the tan leather seats, whose colour was echoed on the door trims, lower dashboard and carpet, lifting the dark space of the standard car. The Momo steering wheel also made way for one of the most desirable pieces ever to see service in an MX-5, a thin, wood-rimmed wheel from Italian maker Nardi. A Nardi gear knob and wood-trimmed handbrake handle completed the retro look.

V-Special models are currently the most desirable used MX-5s on the market, and rarely stay on forecourts or in the classified ads for very long. As a result, you can expect to pay a reasonable amount more for a V-Spec than you would for most other editions in similar condition. Mazda released further V-Special models from 1990 on the Japanese market, featuring black paint rather than Neo Green.

1990 – J-LIMITED (JAPAN)

Rare and sought-after by enthusiasts, Mazda produced only eight hundred Sunburst Yellow J-Limited cars from 1990, based on the special package Japanese model, which included alloy wheels, power steering and electric windows. In addition to these options, the J-Limited boasted the same wooden Nardi steering wheel, wooden gear

The Roadster J-Limited was the first MX-5 to wear vivid yellow paint. MAZDA

knob and wooden handbrake handle found in the V-Special. Stainless steel scuff plates also featured, adding a touch of class over the standard car.

Demand for the J-Limited was so high, that all eight hundred units sold on the first day. Mazda created a J-Limited II model in 1993, with the same colour and equipment levels, but featuring the later seats, a Momo steering wheel and the later alloy wheel design. Again, just eight hundred were produced.

1991 – LIMITED EDITION (UK AND EUROPE)

Though lacking an imaginative title, the Limited Edition was one of the first special MX-5s, and as one of the oldest, it is also particularly rare on today's market. Only 250 were produced for the UK, and it's rumoured that twenty-five of those were reserved for 'tax free sales or personal exports', so even fewer may have actually been sold through dealerships. Each was painted in British Racing Green, differentiating it from the usual white, blue and red standard models. The BBS alloy wheels too were unique, with an upmarket multi-spoke design.

Inside, the Limited Edition was a significant step up from the bare-bones standard model. Tan leather seats and a tan, deep-pile carpet replaced the standard charcoal cloth and thin carpet, and Mazda fitted a wood-rimmed steering wheel, wooden gear knob and wooden handbrake han-

Wooden trim brightened up the otherwise standard J-Limited interior. MAZDA

dle. Owners were granted a few other unique features too, including a leather wallet – fitted with a numbered brass plaque like that was also fitted on the dashboard. The car also came with an embossed key fob and certificate of authenticity.

1991 – 24 HOUR LE MANS (UK)

Mazda enjoyed a special year in 1991. It produced one of motor racing's most iconic images – that of a young Johnny Herbert slumped across the front of his Mazda 787B

Launched in 1991, the MX-5 Le Mans is among the most rare MX-5s of all – just twenty-four were made. MAZDA

The MX-5 Le Mans paint scheme replicated that of the 787B Le Mans-winning racecar. MAZDA

endurance sports car. The British driver had completed the final stints in the car back-to-back, leading him to collapse with exhaustion.

The Le Mans victory marked not only the first for Mazda in the world famous race, and the first for a rotary engine, but also the first for Japan, a feat not repeated, more than two decades later. Mazda decided on the perfect way to celebrate – an extremely limited-edition version of the MX-5, sold only in Herbert's home country, one for every hour of the race that Mazda had been victorious in.

Though based on the regular 1.6-litre car, the Le Mans

was far from standard. It gained the BBR turbocharged conversion to raise performance and also received a body kit. This comprised a slightly redesigned front bumper with a lower lip, wider side skirts, a deeper rear bumper and a rear boot spoiler.

The alloy wheels were taken from the BBR turbo, but most striking of all was the 787B-echoing orange and green patchwork paintwork. For a handful of owners it was a little too conspicuous, so some of the cars were repainted soon after delivery. With only twenty-four units produced, the Le Mans is undoubtedly one of the most rare MX-5 limited edition models.

1992 – S-SPECIAL & S-LIMITED (JAPAN)

S-Special and S-Limited models, sold in Japan only, featured several upgrades to the standard Eunos Roadster. Mazda improved the chassis with Bilstein dampers and a front strut tower brace, while all rode on BBS alloy wheels – gold painted on the S-Limited.

The interior was furnished with a Nardi steering wheel and gear knob, while the S-Limited featured red leather seat trim. Both cars were painted in Brilliant Black, while the S-Special model also touted a rear spoiler. Only five hundred S-Special and 1,000 S-Limited cars were made.

1992 – SE

As with the Limited Edition launched in 1991, Mazda's two SE editions, released between 1992 and 1993, eschewed the back-to-basics feel of the standard MX-5, replacing it with surprising levels of luxury for such a small car. The popularity of the first SE model was so great that Mazda released another 150 units, to add to the first two hundred sold from April 1992.

All 350 SEs were finished in Brilliant Black paint and featured 15in alloy wheels. Those on the first two hundred were a deep-dish, multi-spoke design, while painted seven-spoke alloys were fitted to the final 150. The interior was much the same as on the Limited Edition – tan leather and carpets, with a wooden finish to the three-spoke steering wheel, gear knob and handbrake lever. All cars got stainless steel scuff plates featuring the MX-5 logo. Standard equipment included anti-lock brakes, power steering, an electric aerial and an interior boot release.

1992 – M2-1001 (JAPAN)

While most limited edition models sold in the UK and USA often featured little more than new paint jobs and token trim items to shift end-of-production models, the Japanese market saw a trifecta of special Eunos Roadsters developed by M2 Corporation.

Far from mere cosmetic jobs, the M2 cars – of which the M2-1001 was the first – featured several alterations over the standard Eunos Roadster. Nevertheless, they

The S-Special used distinctive BBS multi-spoke alloy wheels. MAZDA

Inside, the S-Special got an upgraded stereo system and a Nardi wheel. MAZDA

The S-Limited models are among the more distinctive MX-5 editions. MAZDA

were official Eunos models – not that they could be bought at the local Mazda dealership, of course.

As is frequently the way in Japan, demand for the M2-1001 was so high that M2 Corporation held a lottery for the 300 units and prospective customers had to travel to the company's headquarters in Tokyo to put their names on the list.

Based on the regular first-generation NA6 Roadster, each 1001 was given a coat of Blueish Black Mica (also known as Brave Blue Mica) paint and a unique body kit. The kit comprised a larger front air dam with integrated round fog lights and a small tail spoiler mounted on the boot lid. The regular plastic door mirrors were ditched in favour of retro-style chrome bullet mirrors. A metal filler cap replaced the standard fuel flap.

The interior saw significant changes too, from a chrome-plated version of the classic Momo wheel found in regular MX-5s, to an entirely new instrument cluster. This now comprised only four dials – speedometer, tachometer, temperature and fuel – with thick chrome bezels similar to those of a classic vehicle. The warning lights were now small bulbs sprouting from the instrument cluster.

And he changes didn't stop there. The M2-1001 gained bucket seats, sport pedals, a slightly redesigned dashboard facia, a much simpler console between the seats and retro-style door trims. M2 Performance also saw fit to delete the standard air conditioning and electric windows, in order to save weight.

M2's alterations were more than cosmetic, too. Panasport 15x6 alloy wheels replaced the narrower and smaller standard wheels, while the chassis was improved with uprated suspension, a four-point roll bar and a strut brace. Drivers would have to work harder too, with the removal of the power steering system.

The engine received upgraded pistons, a new crankshaft, a lighter flywheel and extra cooling for the limited-slip differential. Breathing was improved with an HKS exhaust system and all these changes resulted in a maximum output of 132bhp, up from the standard 116. Torque increased from 136Nm to 148Nm (100 to 109lb ft).

Contemporary prices for the M2 were around two million Yen, or about £8,900. It is difficult to believe that such a heavily altered car cost so much less than UK buyers were being charged for a standard vehicle. Of course, shrewd Japanese buyers who made it onto the list had little trouble selling their cars for 2.7 million Yen – around £12,000 at the time.

1993 – M2-1002 (JAPAN)

As hinted at in the name, the M2-1002 was the second of M2's special MX-5 projects, this time putting a greater emphasis on luxury. Only three hundred were built, all painted in the same dark metallic shade of blue, Brave Blue Mica.

Based on the 1.6-litre car, the 1002 was highly specified inside and out. Like the 1001, several exterior changes were made, including a re-designed front bumper and a set of 8-spoke, 15in Panasport alloy wheels. The interior was similarly modified – the standard instrument cluster was replaced by a set of retro dials and the armrest and centre console were removed, replaced by a carpeted transmission tunnel.

From here, the 1002 became more luxurious than its predecessor. The interior was trimmed in cream leather, covering everything from the seats and parcel shelf, to the dashboard and door cards. The miniature-Jaguar feel was further enhanced by wooden veneer on the centre console, and wooden gear knob and handbrake levers. The standard plastic pedals and window winders were replaced with aluminium items, a material also found on the under-bonnet strut brace and the bullet-style door mirrors.

1994 – M2-1028 (JAPAN)

Where previous M2 editions of the Eunos Roadster had placed an emphasis on luxury, the third production model took its inspiration from racing vehicles. Some three hundred examples of the M2-1028 were produced from February 1994, aimed at customers wishing to take their Eunos to the track.

The back-to-basics approach started with the colour scheme, with only Chaste White and Brilliant Black available to order. The 1028 was based on the 1.8-litre car, producing 138bhp at 6,500rpm, and 174Nm (123lb ft) of torque at a heady 5,000rpm. The exterior largely matched that of the regular Roadster, with the addition of a front bumper lip and kicked tail to the new aluminium boot lid. A removable hard top also featured and the standard hood was deleted.

M2 also made several changes under the skin, to ensure the car would work on the track. Uprated springs and dampers pulled 15mm (0.6in) closer to the road, and increased roll stiffness 51 per cent at the front and 65 per cent at the rear. A ten-point aluminium roll cage further increased rigidity and safety. The seven-spoke, 14in wheels were wrapped in specially developed Bridgestone RE010 high-performance tyres, enough for a claimed cornering force of up to 0.93g.

Under the bonnet, the engine gained an uprated K&N air filter, a race-spec exhaust header, high-compression pistons that raised compression ratio from 9.0 to 10.6 and a lightened flywheel. A high-lift cam and low back-pressure exhaust were also fitted. Together with significant weight reductions from the lightweight roof, deletion of the centre console, lightweight bucket seats and reduced equipment levels – even the door pulls were replaced by small fabric straps – the 1028 was a much more focused machine than the standard car.

1994 – RS-LIMITED & R-LIMITED (JAPAN)

Based on the S-Special, the RS-Limited was a highly specified model available in Montego Blue Mica. It rode on 15in BBS alloy wheels with Bridgestone RE010 50 tyres. For improved acceleration the RS-Limited had a lower final drive ratio, at 4.3:1. Inside, each car got a three-spoke Nardi steering wheel and impressive one-piece Recaro bucket seats.

Mazda Japan also released the R-Limited in 1994. Similar in specification to the RS-Limited, the R-Limited focused more on luxury, although the lower final drive ratio and lightweight flywheel were used, as was the wheel and tyre package. In addition, the R-Limited featured red leather seats, with red trim on the dashboard, door cards and tonneau cover. A classic wooden Nardi steering wheel, gear knob and handbrake lever were also used. Initially available in Satellite Blue Mica, the R-Limited was later available in Chaste White.

TOP AND ABOVE: *The RS-Limited featured BBS alloy wheels and a pared down interior with bucket seats, Nardi wheel and a chassis brace. MAZDA (BOTH)*

1995 – VR-LIMITED A & B (JAPAN)

The luxurious VR-Limited models sold in Japan were available in two versions as seven hundred units of the Wine Red Mica 'Combination A' and eight hundred units of Excellent Green Mica 'Combination B'. Both were based on the later 1.8-litre S-Special cars. Each was granted a leather

Red leather enlivened the interior of the R-Limited. MAZDA

interior, tan on the red car, black for Combination B, with matching soft tops. A three-spoke steering wheel was standard, as were five-spoke alloy wheels, and aluminium trim on the gear knob, handbrake lever and gear lever surround.

1995 – CALIFORNIA

A buyer in the mid-1990s wishing to stand out in their MX-5 could do no better than the California edition. Built to celebrate the model's fifth anniversary in the UK, the Sunburst Yellow paintwork (known as Speed Yellow in some markets) ensured that the California has become one of the most recognisable special edition MX-5s.

Mazda built three hundred units, based on the standard 1.8 MX-5, between May and October 1995. In addition to the vibrant paintwork, the California also got 15in, five-spoke alloy wheels and low-profile tyres. Inside, it differed little from other MX-5s, so black cloth and sports steering wheel were standard. A California plaque on the dash reminded drivers of the model they had chosen, as if the yellow bonnet stretching ahead wasn't enough of a giveaway.

Mazda sold specials similar to the California in other markets, including the 'Yellow' in Austria, as well as five hundred 'Sunracer' cars in Germany and a further fifty in Switzerland.

1995 – GLENEAGLES

A common theme running through several MX-5 special editions was that of luxury. With basic models catering so well for buyers drawn in by the car's simplicity, Mazda had room at the top of the range to throw in luxury items for more discerning buyers. Few demonstrated this better than the Gleneagles edition, sold between October 1995 and May 1996.

The Gleneagles was based on the standard 1.8-litre model. Mazda made four hundred, all painted in a deep, lustrous Montego Blue. With 15in alloy wheels and Dunlop SP2000 tyres, the car featured exterior Gleneagles badging, in homage to the world famous golf course.

Despite the model costing significantly less than some previous special editions at £16,500, the interior was possibly Mazda's plushest yet in an MX-5. The seats were trimmed with soft champagne leather, which extended to

the door cards and dash pad, and the same colour was used on a new, extended tonneau cover. The centre console and centre tunnel featured walnut-effect trim, while traditional Scottish tartan trim made an appearance on the gear lever gaiter – as well as a special tartan owner's wallet. An expensive-looking four-spoke leather steering wheel finished off the interior makeover.

1996 – VR-LIMITED (JAPAN)

One of the many luxurious takes on the Eunos Roadster, the VR-Limited came in 'Combination A' and 'Combination B' trim levels. The former was painted in Merlot Pearl Clearcoat, with seven hundred examples hitting the Japanese market. The latter was supplied in Excellent Pearl Green Mica, in a run of eight hundred units. Both had leather seats, though the Merlot car was more striking with its tan soft top and cream interior, to the Combination B's dark green soft top and black interior. Aluminium accents enlivened the interiors, with a three-spoke Nardi steering wheel taking centre stage.

1996 – R2 LIMITED (JAPAN)

Based on the already highly specified S-Special Type 1, the R2 Limited was a sporty model available only in white. A red and black leather interior contrasted with the exterior shade, while the 15in, five-spoke alloy wheels wore Bridgestone RE010 50 tyres. Unlike previous editions, this Japanese special gained a driver's airbag in a large, four-spoke steering wheel. Other interior fittings included an aluminium gear knob, handbrake lever and gear lever surround. Only 500 units were produced.

1996 – B2 LIMITED (JAPAN)

Launched alongside the R2 Limited, the B2 model brandished polished alloy wheels and chrome-plated door mirrors, contrasting with a coat of Twilight Blue Mica paint. A dark blue soft top was fitted to match. The interior was largely standard, with a four-spoke, airbag-equipped steering wheel and 'Moquette'-trimmed seats featuring integrated head rests. A double-DIN CD, cassette and radio provided entertainment.

1996 – MONACO (UK)

Based on the newly released 88bhp 1.6, Mazda sold 450 Monaco editions, all painted in British Racing Green. Taking its name from the famous Grand Prix – though photography for the promotional material was done at the historic Brands Hatch circuit in the UK – the Monaco was one of the cheaper MX-5 specials, retailing at £13,750 in 1996.

The cars had 15in alloy wheels and tan-coloured roofs, while the interior saw few changes from the regular 1.6. Monaco badging, with a graphic of the circuit, was fixed to the front wings.

Two late MX-5 special editions – the Monaco and Merlot. MAZDA

The Monaco special edition featured a fairly low specification, but nevertheless proved popular. MAZDA

1996 – MERLOT (UK AND EUROPE)

Like a fine wine, Merlot MX-5s only get better with age and they are now among the more sought-after special editions on the UK market. Sold in a deep metallic red (called both Vin Rouge Mica and Merlot Mica), six hundred Merlot cars were sold across the UK and Europe. They were equipped with unique 15in alloy wheels and high-performance Dunlop SP2000 tyres.

The interior featured several unique features over and above the standard 1.8-litre models. Luxurious grey leather seats took pride of place, finished with burgundy piping. The regular black centre console was fitted with wood-effect trim, a finish replicated on the gear knob and handbrake grip. The first four hundred cars featured a unique leather-trimmed steering wheel, and all had Merlot badging.

1997 – DAKAR (UK)

The Dakar edition of 1997 celebrated the famous Paris–Dakar race, an endurance rally of high attrition that crosses huge sections of Africa. Only four hundred units of the Dakar edition were produced, at £17,210 each. The 1.8-based model was finished in Twilight Blue, with 15in multi-spoke alloy wheels, Dunlop SP Sport tyres and Dakar badging.

Inside, conditions were a little more pleasant than those faced by Dakar crews, with soft grey leather seats with blue piping. A chrome chassis brace curved around the seats, while a Momo steering wheel and burr walnut centre console increased the luxury. Grey, Dakar-branded floor mats were also fitted.

1997 – SR-LIMITED (JAPAN)

One of the last Mk1 special editions, the SR-Limited was typically well equipped and celebrated nine years of production. Only seven hundred units were produced, based on the Japanese M Package models. Cars were available in Sparkle Green Metallic or Chaste White, and all were equipped with polished alloy wheels and a Torsen limited slip differential.

Inside, SR-Limited models featured an airbag steering wheel and black leather seats with light grey nubuck inserts. Each buyer of the SR-Limited was given a unique leather jacket, embroidered with the 'Roadster' logo.

1997 – MONZA (UK)

As with the earlier Monaco edition, the MX-5 might have had little to do with a famous racetrack, but the British Racing Green Monza edition still shared its name with the Italian Grand Prix circuit. A total of eight hundred Monza MX-5s were built between May and September 1997, based on the standard 1.6i car. Monzas featured 14in alloy wheels and the bonnet and each rear wing displayed a winner's wreath-style Monza decal.

1997 – HARVARD (UK)

The luxurious Harvard MX-5, available between May and September 1997, took its name from the famed university in Cambridge, Massachusetts. The Silver Stone Metallic car set the contemporary buyer back by £17,495. For that, they got one of only five hundred cars, each with 15in, five-spoke alloys wrapped in Pirelli P6000 tyres.

Upholstery was in burgundy leather with grey piping. A three-spoke Momo leather steering wheel and walnut effect trim complemented the burgundy floor mats and chrome chassis brace behind the seats. A small burgundy Harvard badge was carried on each front wing.

1997 – MAZDASPEED B-SPEC (JAPAN)

The Japan-only Mazdaspeed B-Spec was a highly tuned special edition, blurring the lines between road car and racer. By fitting an Eaton supercharger to the standard 1.8-litre engine, Mazdaspeed raised power to over 177bhp. Available in a colour of the buyer's choice, each B-Spec also wore an unsubtle body kit to signify its intentions. A deep splitter was added to the front bumper, with side skirts and a rear bumper to match. A huge rear wing and B-Spec decal on the front wing completed the exterior changes. Inside, the regular seats were replaced by large, supportive bucket seats, with red trim.

1998 – BERKELEY (UK)

Last of the Mk1 MX-5 special editions, the Sparkle Green Berkeley is one of the most highly prized UK-market MX-5s. With California to thank for so much of the MX-5's

Mazdaspeed

In common with many Japanese automobile companies, Mazda has long had a dedicated performance division, tasked with extracting the maximum performance from its models. That company is Mazdaspeed. Its story began in 1967, when Japan's largest Mazda dealer, Mazda Auto Tokyo, set up the Mazda Sports Corner racing team.

First working on Mazda's innovative rotary-engined Cosmo, Mazda Sports Corner set about raising Mazda's international racing presence. No more daunting debut could be chosen than an 84-hour endurance marathon at the Nürburgring Nordschleife in West Germany, for the 'Marathon de la Route'. Remarkably, the team scored a fourth-place finish. Further success followed over the next fifteen years, including class wins for the Mazda R100 in the Spa-Francorchamps 24-hour and dozens of victories as the team moved through RX-2s, RX-3s and the new RX-7 sports car.

Mazda Motor Corporation finally recognised the team's success and bought the outfit in 1983, changing its name to Mazdaspeed. Eight years later, Mazdaspeed achieved its greatest ever triumph – victory in the gruelling 59th 24 Heures du Mans, with the Mazda 787B.

Tipping the scales at 830kg (1,830lb) and with a four-rotor, 2616cc engine producing 700bhp, the 787B was unlike anything that had raced at Le Mans before. Its victory I the hands of Bertrand Gachot, Volker Weidler and Johnny Herbert remains Mazda's, a rotary engine's, the 787B's and Japan's sole victory at Circuit de Sarthe.

Mazda took full control of Mazdaspeed in 1999. Since then, it has been responsible for both a huge number of Mazda's performance production vehicles, as well as handling the marque's worldwide racing operations. Mazdaspeed parts are available for virtually all Mazda vehicles and several official Mazdaspeed MX-5s have been produced and enjoyed over the years.

development, the Berkeley took its name from the Californian university and only four hundred units were produced. Each of these featured Berkeley badging beneath the side repeaters, unique 15in alloy wheels, and a standard-fit chrome boot rack. Under the bonnet sat the standard 1.8-litre engine.

On the inside, the Berkeley continued the luxurious theme of other late-model MX-5s. The seats were trimmed in black and grey leather, the grey theme continuing on to the door panels. The centre console was trimmed with a wood-effect finish and the usual MX-5 steering wheel made way for a chunky, leather Momo item. Stainless steel scuff plates and a chromed brace bar completed the interior modifications.

1998 – Mazdaspeed C-Spec (Japan and USA)

Only a handful of Mazdaspeed-tuned C-Spec models were produced, making it among the most rare of MX-5 models. Barely recognisable from the Mk1 MX-5 on which it was based, the C-Spec used heavily modified bodywork for improved aerodynamics, the long nose and tail designs reflecting the trend for similar modifications in GT endurance racing. The front end was completely redesigned, with wider bodywork and faired-in headlamps more similar to those of a Marcos or TVR. The entire front end was of a clamshell design, hinging forwards for access to the engine. The back end was also unrecognisable from the standard Mk1, with wider arches, redesigned rear lights and a longer profile. Only the doors remained unchanged.

A bored-out 1995cc unit replaced the standard 1.8-litre engine. Tuning raised output to 197bhp at 7,900rpm, and 200.9Nm (148.2lb ft) of torque from 5,000rpm. And although the bodywork additions made the car look larger and heavier, a kerb weight of just 1009kg (2,224lb) ensured rapid performance.

The interior was largely that of the standard MX-5, but completely re-trimmed. One car, with blue metallic paint on the exterior, was re-trimmed in cream-coloured leather for a more expensive ambience. Even the dials, steering wheel, gear lever and handbrake handle were cream-coloured, while the plastic centre console was removed and replaced by a cream-coloured carpet. These cars cost the equivalent of over £40,000 at the time, making their rarity unsurprising.

1998 – MAZDASPEED A-SPEC (JAPAN AND USA)

Shortly after the Mk2 MX-5 was launched, customers in Japan and the USA could choose from a wide range of performance parts from official tuner Mazdaspeed. The A-Spec Touring Kit was less of an acquired taste than the C-Spec had been, but the list of available parts was long. Buyers could add to the exterior styling with front and rear bumpers, side skirts, spoilers and headlight covers. Garish three-spoke alloy wheels could also be specified, as could a lightweight fibreglass hard top.

Customers could essentially pick and choose their level of tuning from the Mazdaspeed brochure, or a full kit could be bought with the brand new vehicle. Other Mazdaspeed parts included front and rear springs and dampers, clutch and flywheel kits, a 4-2-1 exhaust manifold, air filters and exhaust systems.

1998 – SPORT (UK)

The first of the Mk2 MX-5 special editions in the UK, the Sport was based on the already-sporty 1.8iS. Only six hundred went on sale, between December 1998 and December 1999, three hundred in Classic Red and the rest in Racing Blue. At £22,535, it is one of the most expensive MX-5s to have gone on sale, but its extensive equipment justified the price.

The exterior wore a fully body kit, including a front spoiler, integrated front fog lamps, large side skirts and a boot spoiler. In addition, the car featured colour-coded rear mud flaps, 15in alloy wheels and a colour-coded detachable hard top. Inside, the black leather seats and Nardi leather wheel were joined by rather incongruous wood-effect centre console trim, while the gear knob and handbrake grip were also trimmed in wood.

The rare Sport MX-5 kicked off a long line of Mk2 special editions. MAZDA

1999 – 10TH ANNIVERSARY EDITION (WORLDWIDE)

For MX-5 enthusiasts, the 10th Anniversary Edition is one of the most well-known and sought-after models. Arriving only shortly after the introduction of the Mk2 MX-5 in 1998, the 10th Anniversary Edition celebrated a decade since the first MX-5s had rolled off the production line and buyers in Europe, North America, Japan and Australia were treated to a raft of special features and mechanical upgrades, many of which had not been seen on the standard models in most markets.

Most noticeable at a glance was the Sapphire Blue Mica paintwork, complemented by chrome-finished versions of the standard car's 15in wheels. A small badge on the driver's side quarter panel denoted the edition and model number, out of the 7,500 units produced.

The interior gained a mixture of black leather and blue Alcantara trim for the seats, as well as a blue gear lever gaiter, blue carpets and blue dials. The Nardi airbag steering wheel was wrapped in blue leather, while the blue floor mats were emblazoned with the 10th Anniversary logo and the centre console had carbon fibre-style trim.

Where the visual alterations ended, the mechanical changes began. Although the 10th Anniversary Edition was based on the familiar 1.8-litre car, markets outside Japan were granted a six-speed gearbox for the first time. This actually made the quoted acceleration figures for the car slower than with the five-speed gearbox, as a result of the driver needing an extra gear change before 62mph. Contemporary road tests were positive about the upgrade, however, citing a greater ability to keep the engine on the boil.

Mazda gave the chassis some careful attention too. The installation of a stiffer anti-roll bar and a set of Bilstein shock absorbers tightened up the handling, without compromising on ride quality.

One of the best recognised MX-5s is the 10th Anniversary Edition, sold worldwide. MAZDA

The 10th Anniversary Edition featured blue trim, plus a six-speed manual gearbox. MAZDA

2000 – CALIFORNIA

In keeping with the 1995 California edition of the Mk1, a bright Sunburst Yellow paint job placed the Mk2 California among the less subtle MX-5 limited editions. It was based on the entry-level 1.6 and exterior changes were limited to the paint shade and California badging, as well as a set of 15in alloy wheels in a different design to that found on the regular car. Interior changes were restricted to special yellow and black California floor mats.

Though mechanically unchanged, the California, thanks mainly to its vivid hue, is considered one of the more sought after Mk2 MX-5s and tends to command slightly higher prices on the used market.

While the first California edition used a 1.8-litre engine, the Mk2 was based on the standard 1.6 MX-5. MAZDA

2000 – JASPER CONRAN (UK)

Some cars benefit from the input of designers in the world of fashion, such as the Mary Quant and Paul Smith classic Minis, or the Jasper Conran MX-5, launched on the UK market in 2000. Only five hundred were produced, with one hundred in Platinum Silver and the rest in Classic Black. Based on the 1.8iS, the cars featured a series of details selected by Conran. Exterior changes were limited to the paint shades, a new 15in alloy wheel design by BBS, satin silver exhaust trim, sports suspension and unique badges.

Inside, the changes were more comprehensive. Typical of many limited edition MX-5s over the years, leather trim was central to the changes. In this instance, soft Connolly leather covered the seats and hood cover – black in the black cars, red in the rare silver model. Wilton carpets were coloured to match and even used to trim the boot. A set of Jasper Conran luggage was also supplied.

Aluminium-effect trim was splashed liberally about the cabin, on the centre console, vent rings, the gear knob, handbrake lever and door pulls, as well as on the part-leather steering wheel. A very 'of the time' MiniDisc and CD player was also included.

While the black Jasper Conran model retailed for £21,000, the silver version had a price tag of £24,000 – winning it the unique accolade of being the most expensive series MX-5 ever sold.

Top designer Jasper Conran added his personal touch to the Conran special edition. MAZDA

2001 – MAZDA ROADSTER MPS (JAPAN)

Initially released as a concept at the Tokyo Motor Show in 2001, Mazda soon saw fit to put the Roadster MPS into limited-run production for the Japanese home market. Created by Mazdaspeed, the Roadster MPS was a very different animal to the Mazdaspeed Miata released a few years later in North America. While that car was turbocharged and otherwise fairly standard, the MPS featured a heavily modified version of the standard 1839cc naturally aspirated engine.

With the new in-house designation BP-VE, Mazdaspeed enlarged the engine's capacity to 2.0-litres by increasing both bore and stroke. Power increased to a lively 197hp at 7,000rpm, with peak torque of 197Nm (145lb ft) developed at a screaming 6,000rpm. To achieve these numbers, the BP-VE engine was fitted with individual throttle bodies for each port and high-lift cams. Although the engine was far from standard, Mazda used the regular car's six-speed manual transmission.

The exterior was notably different from that of the regular Mk2, with an entirely redesigned front bumper. As well as including an extra air intake on its upper edge, the lower grille was now larger and flanked by two extra ducts for brake cooling. Individual headlights set deep into the bumper replaced the standard units, while smooth Perspex covers improved aerodynamics. The rear bumper was also changed to improve aerodynamics.

To accommodate a 50mm (2in) wider front track and 60mm (2.4in) wider rear track, the MPS also featured flared wheel arches, not dissimilar to those now found on Mk3 MX-5s. It rode on 17x7in, five-spoke alloy wheels, wrapped in 215/40 R17 Michelin Pilot tyres. Ventilated discs at the front and solid at the rear, all 314mm (12.4in) in diameter, handled braking.

Chassis rigidity was improved with an aluminium ladder structure down the length of the underbody, while a three-point strut and bulkhead brace reduced flex under the bonnet. These alterations allowed the height-adjustable mono-tube dampers and uprated coil springs to increase the car's agility.

Changes to the interior were more limited, with a standard dashboard and centre console. The standard seats were re-profiled for better support and upholstered in leather and Alcantara. The standard three-spoke steering wheel also featured both materials. Mazda produced only two hundred units and the car's price was quoted at between 3.5 and 4.5 million Yen – £20,250 to £26,000 at the time.

The Mazda Roadster MPS, seen here in sketch form. MAZDA

The Mazda MPS roadster was highly tuned, with a bored-out 2.0-litre engine producing 197bhp. MAZDA

2000 – ICON (UK)

It speaks of Mazda's confidence in the MX-5 that it can name one of its special editions 'Icon'. Each of the 750 specials so named was typically well equipped. The exterior was finished in Art Vin Mica, a deep, metallic red shade, while retaining the 15in wheels of the 1.8iS model on which the Icon was based. Inside, beige leather seats and beige on the lower dash, door trims and centre console contrasted with the red paint, as did the cream dials. The steering wheel featured a mahogany finish and wood trim appeared on the gear knob, handbrake lever and centre console.

The Icon – an understated and luxurious special edition. MAZDA

2000 – ISOLA (UK)

Given some of the previous MX-5 special editions and their unique features, the Isola offered little over the standard 1.6 model on which it was based. All five hundred units sported Classic Red paint, with a colour-coded hard top. The exterior touches were completed y 14in alloy wheels, while inside there were no changes over the standard model's cloth seats and black trim.

2001 – MAZDASPEED ROADSTER (JAPAN)

One of the more distinctive MX-5 specials, the Japanese-market Mazdaspeed Roadster was finished in Starry Blue Mica, with contrasting gold-painted wheels. Based on the 1.8-litre RS model, the Mazdaspeed package added four-way adjustable dampers and a body-colour strut tower brace to improve handling. A custom Mazdaspeed exhaust manifold and back box helped increase power, while reinforced engine mounts stabilised the engine under hard acceleration so that more power could be transferred to the road.

The Isola special edition featured an unusually low specification. MAZDA

Other changes to the base RS included extra noise damping, a front air dam, side skirts, rear bumper skirt and rear spoiler. Headlamp covers were also included, as was a Mazdaspeed decal. Inside, the Mazdaspeed got blue, chrome-ringed dials, carbon fibre-style centre console trim, blue stitching on the seats, steering wheel and gear knob, and a blue gaiter for the gear lever.

The vivid blue Mazdaspeed Roadster. MAZDA

2002 – NR-A (JAPAN)

The stripped-out NR-A Roadster was designed as a track-ready toy, inspired by Mazda's Roadster Cup series of the time. With a host of colours available, Mazda offered a long list of accessories to turn the 1.6-engined model into a car suitable for track day and racing enthusiasts.

Standard specification included uprated Bilstein suspension, a limited-slip differential, engine mount reinforcements, a strut tower brace and upgraded brakes. NR-As also got incredibly lightweight 15in Enkei alloy wheels (painted white), and the interior was finished with red seats and a red-trimmed Nardi steering wheel.

Optional extras to make the NR-A even more suitable for track use included a six-point roll cage, red Mazdaspeed bucket seats with four-point racing harnesses, tow hooks, upgraded brake pads and upgraded clutch parts. Prices started at 2,048,000 Yen, around £11,640 in 2002.

Japan's NR-A Roadster was designed for racing and could be optioned with a full roll cage. MAZDA

Inside, the NR-A had sporty red seats and basic equipment levels. MAZDA

2002 – PHOENIX (UK AND GERMANY)

Mazda made 1,200 units of the MX-5 Phoenix, making it one of the more common special editions. Both 1.6 and 1.8-litre versions were available, retailing for £15,995 and £16,995, respectively, from March 2002.

Brilliant Black paintwork was standard, but buyers could also specify Titanium Grey Mica finish at extra cost. Lightweight, 15in Enkei alloy wheels were fitted, while buyers could opt for a metal-finished style bar and wind blocker to improve the car's looks when roofless. Inside, the seats, door cards and Nardi steering wheel were wrapped in sienna brown leather, while black leather covered the gear knob and handbrake lever. Alloy-effect trim accents enlivened the dashboard and instrument bezels, and an upgraded CD player with extra speakers provided the tunes.

2002 – ARIZONA

Buyers who managed to miss the vivid yellow California edition in 2000 had another chance from June to November 2002, with a Blazda Yellow Mica option on the Arizona edition. Cars were also supplied in Eternal Red and Sunlight Silver shades, while customers could choose between 1.6 and 1.8-litre engines.

The cars were fitted with 15in Enkei alloy wheels and their tasteful interior design featured black leather heated seats, with the same material on the steering wheel, hand brake lever and gear knob. Alloy-effect trim could be found on the dashboard, air vent bezels and instrument surrounds, a shade echoed on the style bar found behind the seats. Arizona mats, with edging coloured to match the exterior colour, were available to enliven the dark interior further.

2002 – TRILOGY (UK)

A standout aspect of the Trilogy edition wasn't found on the car itself, but in the special key ring that was gifted to every owner. Formed from solid silver, remarkably each key ring contained three 0.5-carat diamonds. The name of this edition, Trilogy, is a trademark of the De Beers diamond company and refers to just such an arrangement in its jewellery.

Continuing the Trilogy theme, only 333 units were built, based on the standard 1.8-litre car and painted in Brilliant Black. Chrome-finished 15in alloy wheels were fitted, while unique Trilogy badging found its way onto each front wing and the chrome scuff plates. Inside, the seats were trimmed in luxury grey Medici leather and featured a stitched Trilogy logo. A two-tone Nardi leather steering wheel, leather gear knob and handbrake grip completed the luxury look.

2002 – MONTANA (UK)

October 2002 saw the launch of the £18,995 MX-5 Montana, the five hundred units of which were based on the 1800cc model. Some 250 were painted in Garnet Red, while the rest were finished in Racing Green. A mohair soft top was standard, but all Montanas were also sold with a colour-coded detachable hard top. Standard fog lamps and 15in alloy wheels completed the exterior look.

Inside, each car featured tan leather heated seats and a tan carpet. Wooden trim was included for the first time since the Icon, covering the steering wheel rim, gear knob and hand brake handle. Wood-effect trim also found its way onto the centre console, while chrome trim brightened up the interior door handles and speaker grilles.

2003 – NEVADA

Mazda built 2,050 of the Nevada edition between February and March 2003, in several versions. Colour choice was split between Cerion Silver and Strato Blue, while buyers could choose between the 1.6 engine (200 in silver, 100 in blue), 1.8 with a cloth-trimmed interior (370 silver, 190 blue) or a higher-spec 1.8 with leather trim (780 silver, 410 blue).

All included 15in alloy wheels with low-profile tyres and a colour-coded soft-top. Inside, the colour choices were reversed, silver cars sporting a blue interior and blue cars being trimmed in grey. The gear knob featured a leather finish, while the steering wheel was trimmed in two-tone leather. Aluminium-effect trim covered the centre console and air vent bezels.

2003 – ANGELS (UK)

Celebrity endorsement is frequently used to sell a few extra vehicles, but film-themed vehicles are thankfully a lot less common. The 2003 MX-5 Angels is an exception, sold to coincide with the 2003 film *Charlie's Angels – Full Throttle*. Predictably, an MX-5 doesn't feature in the movie, but 500 lucky customers would have the option of the highly specified car.

Mazda built 1.6 and 1.8-litre versions, with 61 and 114 units of each painted Eternal Red, and 114 and 211 units of each engine in Sunlight Silver. Angels badging, 15in alloy wheels and a rear boot spoiler completed the exterior changes. Inside, Mazda trimmed each car in black leather with red stitching, while chrome trim lined the centre console and vent rings. Angels-badged stainless steel scuff plates and style bars were also included. Prices started at £16,500 for the 1.6.

2003 – INDIANA (UK)

With only 250 units made, the Indiana is among the less common MX-5 specials. Based on the standard 1.8, all were finished in Garnet Red Metallic paint. The specification was high, with front fog lamps, 15in alloy wheels, a beige leather interior and mahogany wood trim on the steering wheel, gear knob, handbrake and centre console.

The lower dash, centre console and door trims were trimmed in matching beige, and chrome accents finished several interior fittings. The Indiana model cost £17,000.

2004 – EUPHONIC (UK)

The MX-5 Euphonic was all about sound – music, rather than the car's sporty exhaust note. Priced at £16,500 for the 1.6 and £17,000 for the 1.8, the Euphonic came with a high-spec Sony CDX-MP80 MP3/CD radio head unit, with a Sony CDX-T69 six-CD autochanger mounted in the boot. Via a remote control, buyers could pump music through a six-speaker system, with tweeters and 150W X-Plod speakers in each door, and two 25W speakers in the windblocker, behind the driver and passenger.

In addition, the car got 16in alloy wheels finished in Mesh Titanium paint and the option of Brilliant Black, Titanium Grey, Velocity Red and Sunlight Silver paint. Two thousand units were produced, all featuring a black leather interior and carbon-fibre effect centre console.

2004 – MAZDASPEED (USA)

If there has been one recurring complaint about the MX-5, it is about the car's perceived lack of performance. Indeed, Mazda granted the MX-5 such a capable chassis that it's always had the potential to handle much more power.

While UK buyers were given the BBR Turbo option soon after the car's launch, it took until 2004 for US buyers to benefit from the same factory-warranted option, this time in the form of the Mazdaspeed Miata. Several,

America's Mazdaspeed Miata gave US customers a dose of turbocharged fun. MAZDA

very limited, tuned MX-5s had already been sold by Mazdaspeed, but North America's car was much less extreme, enhancing the existing car rather than turning it into a track-focused machine.

Key to the conversion was the turbocharger, which allowed the 1.8-litre engine to develop 178hp at 6,000rpm and raised torque to 225Nm (166lb ft) at 4,500rpm. An air-to-air intercooler ensured the engine received cold, fresh air and the engine's cooling systems were uprated to suit the new power output. A heavy-duty clutch, heavy-duty driveshafts and a torque-sensing limited-slip differential helped transfer the extra power to the asphalt; the exhaust note was enhanced by a stainless steel Mazdaspeed exhaust system.

The exterior and chassis saw changes too. Wide 205-section tyres were wrapped around 17in Racing Hart alloy wheels and the car sat lower on Mazdaspeed-tuned Bilstein suspension. Only two colours were available, Velocity Red Mica and Titanium Grey Metallic, and the styling was further enhanced by unique touches including front and rear air dams, and a small rear spoiler. Adding to the more aggressive look, the headlight housings gained a 'smoke' tint.

Many drivers felt the Mazdaspeed had finally exploited the MX-5's potential, with no degradation in the great handling, but a power to weight ratio that – as Mazda boasted in its brochure – now put it on par with the more expensive BMW Z4 2.5.

2004 – ARCTIC

Mazda produced 2,000 of the Arctic edition from August 2004, painted in Razor Blue, Titanium Grey or Sunlight Silver. Customers could choose between the 1.6 for £17,000 and the 1.8 at £17,500. All came with a blue fabric soft top, chrome window trims and 15in alloy wheels.

Inside were blue leather seats and matching door panels, with a black leather steering wheel rim, gear knob and handbrake grip. Silver-finish trim covered the stereo and centre console.

2005 – ICON

Not a company to shy away from its own success, Mazda returned to the Icon name to describe its final Mk2 MX-5. Two engines were available – a 1.6 priced at £16,600 and

the variable valve timing-equipped 1.8 at £17,100. Icons were painted in Black Mica, Titanium Grey or Sunlight Silver, with a vivid Chilli Orange also available and featured in Mazda's promotional material.

The cars boasted 15in Enkei alloy wheels and low-profile tyres, while black leather seats with orange stitching graced the interior. The steering wheel, gear knob and handbrake grip were similarly finished, and silver trim brightened up the centre console, vent rings and instruments. As with the Euphonic, a special sound board mounted to the style bar housed two extra speakers for the single-CD stereo system. To sweeten the deal, each customer received a £500 gift voucher from Mazda, to be spent on genuine Mazda Accessories.

2005 – LAUNCH EDITION (WORLDWIDE)

Mazda produced 7,500 of the Launch Edition model of the new third-generation MX-5. Sold worldwide, three hundred units made it to UK shores, costing £19,999 each. They sported Velocity Red paintwork and special 17in alloy wheels, while a chrome-finish windscreen surround joined similarly finished door handles, fog lamp rings and front grille.

The interior was trimmed in black and red leather, with matching door trim panels. Aluminium-effect trim could be found on the central dashboard panel, steering wheel, style bars and speaker grilles, while the air vent bezels and dials gained chrome rings. As usual, the steering wheel, gear knob and handbrake grip were all trimmed in black leather. Buyers could also enjoy a six-CD, seven-speaker Bose sound system. Each car featured a numbered plaque just forward of the gearstick, denoting its place in the 3,500-car production run.

2006 – NR-A ROADSTER (JAPAN)

Mazda announced the launch of a race-ready NR-A Roadster once again in April 2006. As with the previous Mk2 NR-A, the car was fairly basic, but provided budding racers with the ideal base vehicle to turn into a racecar.

Now based on the range-topping 2.0-litre model, the NR-A concentrated on offering useful equipment, rather than luxurious touches. Height-adjustable Bil-

Like the Mk2 NR-A, the Mk3 was aimed primarily at owners wishing to go racing. MAZDA

stein dampers came as standard, as did a Torsen limited-slip differential. A front suspension strut brace was also fitted. Mazda understood that most racers will change their wheels and tyres, so the standard NR-A cars came only with 16in steel wheels, like those otherwise fitted only to base-model MX-5s in Europe. A five-speed manual transmission, rather than the six-speed, was standard.

The NR-A was designed to compete in the 'Roadster Party' one-make race series in Japan. The events were organised and sponsored by Mazda, and began in September 2006.

2007 – Z-SPORT (UK)

Lavish equipment levels and a £19,999 price tag marked the Z-Sport edition out from the regular 2.0i Sport. All four hundred units were painted in Radiant Ebony Mica, while chrome detailing highlighted the door handles, headlamp units and front bumper grille. All featured standard front fog lamps. Further embellishing the expensive exterior look, the Z-Sport rolled on 17in BBS alloy wheels.

Inside, the Z-Sport was trimmed in stone-coloured leather with matching door trim panels. The dashboard shone with aluminium accents, as did the door speaker grilles, air vent bezels and steering wheel. The wheel, handbrake lever and gear knob were trimmed in leather, while the dials featured chrome rings.

2007 – ICON (UK)

Another generation of MX-5, brought another Icon model to show off the car's success. With Copper Red, Marble White and Stormy Blue Mica paint options, the latest Icon gave a little nod to the colours available on the very first MX-5s, albeit with a slightly more luxurious appearance.

Mazda built 875 units of the £16,825 1.8-litre model and 375 of the 2.0, which retailed for £17,825. Both were based on standard MX-5 models and included 16in alloy wheels, a chrome style bar and front fog lamps. Inside, the Icon exhibited black leather trim, with the word 'Icon' stitched into the headrests. Black leather could also be found on the door panels, while aluminium and chrome effect parts brightened up various aspects of the interior.

2008 – NISEKO (UK)

Niseko is an area of the Hokkaido region in Japan, popular for its mountains and ski resorts; brochure images for the MX-5 Niseko played heavily on the mountainous theme. The cars were available in crisp Icy Blue and Sunlight Silver paint finishes, and Mazda built 240 with the 1.8-litre engine and soft top, and 560 hardtop, 2.0-litre models.

The former set buyers back £17,995 in January 2008, the latter £19,995. Both were well equipped, adding front fog lamps, 17in alloy wheels and chrome accents to the exterior specification. Chrome featured on the door handles, side marker rings, headlamp and fog lamp units, and the front grille.

Inside, the seats, handbrake lever, gear knob, door panels and steering wheel were trimmed in dark brown leather with light blue stitching. Style bar trims were painted to match the exterior body colour, while unique Niseko-stitched floor mats also made an appearance.

2009 – ROADSTER 20TH ANNIVERSARY (JAPAN)

Twenty years since the MX-5 had been unveiled at the Chicago Auto Show, Mazda commemorated the event with a special edition for the Japanese market. The Mazda

Roadster 20th Anniversary hit Japanese dealerships in July 2009, specified to a high standard.

The 20th Anniversary models were based on the Roadster RS soft-top and Roadster VS Power Retractable Hard Top (RHT) sold in Japan. The soft-top models used a six-speed manual transmission, while the RHT cars had the six-speed auto. All were painted in Crystal White Pearl Mica and designated by exterior badging celebrating the MX-5's anniversary. Other special equipment included 17in alloy wheels, clear front fog lights and coloured fog lamp bezels.

All the Anniversary cars had special Recaro bucket seats, trimmed in black Alcantara and red leather. They were also heated, with five temperature settings, while the centre console lid and door armrests gained soft synthetic leather padding. The cars were priced from 2,860,000 Yen, around £18,100.

2010 – 20TH ANNIVERSARY EDITION (UK)

The MX-5's official 20th anniversary had taken place a year earlier in Japan and the US, but in the UK, 2010 marked twenty years of MX-5 sales. To celebrate, Mazda UK created its own 20th Anniversary Edition (AE). Based on the facelifted version of the Mk3 car, it took things back to basics.

To the surprise of many, the 20th AE used the basic car's 1.8-litre engine, rather than the more powerful 2.0-litre unit. The idea was to replicate the true spirit of the original, although the equipment levels would still be alien to owners of the early Mk1. The 20th AE cost just £55 more than the 1.8 SE on which it was based, but included £650 of extra equipment.

Upgrades included 17in, ten-spoke alloy wheels, front fog lights, chrome trim, body-coloured roll bars and a matching strut brace. On the inside, buyers enjoyed a body-coloured dashboard insert, aluminium pedals, stainless steel scuff plates and air conditioning. The obligatory '20th Anniversary' numbered badge was also included.

In homage to the original car, the 20th Anniversary Edition was sold in only three colours – True Red, Crystal White Pearlescent and Aurora Blue Mica. Brave buyers could even specify the white car with red and blue race-style decals.

2010 – MIYAKO (UK)

Mazda launched the Miyako edition as part of its ongoing MX-5 20th anniversary celebrations. A little more subtle than the 20th Anniversary Edition, it was sold from July 2010 and available as both a 1.8-litre model with the soft-top roof and a more powerful 2.0 Roadster Coupé. The former was priced from £18,385 on the road, the latter at £20,885. Five hundred examples of each were produced.

Billed as a 'summer special edition', the Miyako was named after the idyllic Japanese holiday island of Miyako-jima. Home to some of the most beautiful spots in Japan, Mazda calls it the perfect location for open-top motoring – perfect, one would assume, for a new MX-5. Both versions of the car were launched in Aluminium Silver Metallic paint, with Velocity Red Mica also available on the soft-top car.

Aside from the paintwork, only standard front fog lamps and 17in alloy wheels marked out Miyakos from regular MX-5s, while inside the seats were trimmed with Medici premium perforated black leather with red underlay and stitching. The Miyako also gained climate control, unique floor mats and special badging.

2011 – KENDO (UK)

Famous locations were often a theme for Mk1 special editions, while several Mk2s were named after US states and if there is a theme for Mk3 editions, it's Japanese culture. The Kendo was named after the modern-day Japanese martial art of sword fighting, and translates roughly as 'the way of the sword'. It's all about fighting spirit, eye-catching dynamic movement and refinement – all qualities one might recognise in the MX-5.

Continuing another common theme, the Kendo cars were available in 1.8 soft-top and 2.0 Roadster Coupé versions, in Sparkling Black or Dolphin Grey. They were distinguished by 17in alloy wheels, unique exterior badging and fog lamps. Inside, they featured stone grey leather trim, grey stitching on the steering wheel and handbrake, heated seats, a brushed aluminium style bar trim and aluminium pedals.

A Bose audio system was standard and Kendo models cost from £19,255 to £22,320. The MX-5 Kendo edition also celebrated another milestone in the model's history – 900,000 units sold worldwide and more than 100,000 sold in the UK.

The Miyako edition was available in metallic grey, or Red Mica paint. MAZDA

2011 – SPORT BLACK (UK)

Taking a break from Japanese-themed editions, the Sport Black celebrated something closer to home – Mazda and Jota Sport's endurance-racing MX-5. Sharing its Spirited Green metallic paint with the racer, the Sport Black could also be ordered in Velocity Red or Crystal White – though not in black.

Instead, the Sport Tech Roadster Coupé-based model featured a black hardtop roof, dark gunmetal 17in alloy wheels and black door mirrors. Each wing also sported a small Sport Black badge above the side repeater. Inside, the Sport Black got unique floor mats, stainless steel scuff plates, alloy pedals and a black dash panel. Seats, steering wheel and handbrake lever were all trimmed in black leather. Mazda produced a total of five hundred Sport Black cars, at £22,995 each.

The Mk3.5 MX-5 Sport Black – more green than black. MAZDA

2012 – VENTURE (UK)

The MX-5 Venture edition was probably one of the highest-specified MX-5s ever. Based on the 1.8 and 2.0 models, fitted with the soft top and retractable hardtop, respectively, the Venture featured a standard-fit Sanyo TomTom satellite navigation system, with a 147mm (5.8in) touchscreen integrated into the dashboard. The system also incorporated Bluetooth and iPod compatibility, so few Venture drivers are likely to get either lost or bored!

Inside, the leather steering wheel, gear knob and handbrake lever complement the Havana Brown leather heated seats, while the dashboard and steering wheel are both trimmed with piano black inserts.

On the outside, drivers could choose between the exotically named colours Radiant Ebony Mica, Crystal White Pearlescent or Metropolitan Grey Mica paintwork, while chrome-finish inserts reflect the luxury available inside. Gunmetal-coloured 17in alloy wheels and Venture badging completed the look.

The luxurious Venture edition featured a central touchscreen display. ANTONY INGRAM

2012 – KURO (UK)

Kuro is the Japanese word for black, so naturally, as well as Crystal White Pearlescent and Velocity Red Mica, Mazda's colour-dedicated special edition was also available in Brilliant Black. Based on both the 1.8- and 2.0-litre models, the Kuro was distinguished by 17in gunmetal-finish alloy wheels, black mirror surrounds and a black roof, as either the soft-top or retractable hardtop. At the front, the model was equipped with standard fog lights and a mesh grille, while the rear bumper gained a diffuser-style fitting, with larger twin exhaust trims. Most distinctive were the red and grey racing stripes finishing each door, with a chequered flag motif and Kuro lettering. A chrome Kuro badge finished off each front wing.

Inside, the car is typically well equipped, in common with the majority of later MX-5 specials. The heated seats are finished in stone grey and black leather with red stitching, which also features on the door cards. The central dashboard panel has a dark silver finish with red accents, with high-quality, Kuro-badged floor mats finishing the look.

With racing stripes and bright red paintwork, the Kuro edition certainly stands out. ANTONY INGRAM

Kuro models could be specified as either a 1.8-litre soft tops, or a 2.0-litre Roadster Coupés. ANTONY INGRAM

ABOVE: *Inside, the Kuro has grey leather seats and red accents.*
ANTONY INGRAM

RIGHT: *The Kuro's red accents also surround its air vent bezels.*
ANTONY INGRAM

2012 – MX-5 SENSHU (EUROPE)

The MX-5 Senshu hit the auto show stands in 2012, debuting at the Leipzig Motor Show. Alongside the more potent Yusho, a prototype designed to show off Mazda's performance capabilities, the Senshu was a standard special edition, but a rare one, with only two hundred units produced for the European market. Cars were available in white, Brilliant Black Metallic, and Tornado Red.

They were based on the standard 2.0-litre, 158hp model, with the retractable hard top option, 17in alloy wheels matching those of the Yusho and 30mm (1.2in)-lower Bilstein sport suspension. The cars also carried a racing stripe, black rear diffuser, sport exhaust tailpipes and a black bezel for the front grille. Light grey leather seats adorned the interior.

Uniquely, the name was decided by public vote. German TV station DMAX allowed users to vote via Facebook, and after 9,600 votes were cast, 49 per cent chose Senshu. Other naming options included Arashi and Migoto. Three lucky voters were also invited to the Hockenheim race circuit to experience the new MX-5.

CHAPTER 11

CONCEPT CARS AND PROTOTYPES

Mazda's roadster has played host to several prototypes and concept versions over the years. Often these were designed to suggest the direction of future performance models, and occasionally to preview an all-new car entirely. None of the vehicles have yet reached production in their original forms, but many have inspired features on subsequent road models and contribute towards the rich, varied tapestry of Mazda's most famous product. Some have certainly inspired production models – the limited run of Coupé MX-5s in Japan stemmed from original coupé proposals – but most are simply to be enjoyed visually and to inspire future MX-5 owners. As Mazda's road cars develop, it may not be unusual to see some of those concept touches reach the road.

1989 – MAZDA MIATA CLUB SPORT

If the regular MX-5 created a stir upon its 1989 Chicago Auto Show debut, then visitors must really have gaped at the Miata Club Sport displayed alongside it. This one-off, custom version of the newly launched roadster would have been hard to miss in its banana yellow paintwork and matching eight-spoke alloy wheels. Designed at Mazda's Californian design studio, the Club Sport hinted at what a race-prepared Miata might look like – before the first real MX-5 racers hit the track. The front and rear wings were extended by 51mm (2in) to accommodate the fatter wheels and tyres, and the front bumper was widened and deepened to neatly integrate with the new arches.

With high performance, the Miata Club Sport gave press and public alike an idea of the car's potential at Chicago, in 1989. MAZDA

The standard car's pop-up, round headlamps were replaced by small light units under bonnet-level plexiglass covers, improving aerodynamics. Also contributing to the car's race-ready stance was a body-coloured hard tonneau cover and a wide lip spoiler across the boot lid. The studio also removed the passenger door mirror, reducing the car's frontal area. The interior remained largely standard, with only re-trimmed seats, with yellow-stitched Miata logos marking it out from the standard vehicle. It may never have gone into production, but the concept showed that Mazda understood the car's potential at a very early stage.

1995 – MAZDA MIATA M SPEEDSTER

Mazda USA's Miata Speedster concept could never be described as low key, every inch of its ruby-red bodywork suggesting speed, even when standing still. While individual changes to the shape are only slight, their combined differences turned the MX-5 from cute roadster into tarmac-sniffing racer.

At the front, an otherwise standard-looking bumper was augmented by two huge auxiliary lamps, which appeared to have been sourced from a rally car. These fed into widened front and rear arches, giving the car's lines a more muscular stance. A boot lid spoiler and deeper rear valance completed the lower bodywork modifications, but changes to the upper surface were much more pronounced. A plexi-

glass windscreen looked like it was half the height of the standard screen, and a hump behind each seat displaced the usual roof stowage area. One curious change was that the standard side mirrors were flipped upside-down and fitted on the opposite side of the car to their usual position.

The 15x7in TSW Stealth alloy wheels used now look distinctly dated, but riding on 215/50 ZR15 Yokohama AVS tyres, they were as much for purpose as they were for looks. The Speedster rode 38mm (1.5in) lower than the standard car, on custom springs and Koni shocks, and track was widened 13mm (0.5in) to fill the wider arches.

The engine modifications were also significant. The standard 1.8-litre engine was equipped with a Lysholm-type supercharger with an air-to-air intercooler. Engine internals were upgraded with ceramic-coated pistons and a balanced crank, while every aspect of the engine was blueprinted for optimum tolerances. The standard gearbox remained, but a high-performance clutch was fitted. The end result of those modifications was 200hp at 7,000rpm, and 224Nm (165lb ft) of torque at 5,500rpm.

Motor Trend magazine, driving the car in 1996, described it as initially lethargic at low revs, but better as engine revolutions increased. Officially, the Speedster would reach 60mph in 6.8 seconds, and cover the quarter mile in 15.1 seconds. Testers suggested that the prototype was a handful to drive, but in the end Mazda never realised the potential of the M Speedster, despite receiving over 5,000 phone calls from enthusiasts interested in the car.

Mazda's American team made the eye-catching M Speedster, one of the more potent MX-5 concepts. MAZDA

MX-5 Goes Green – Alternative Fuels

As the first decade of the new millennium drew to a close, major car manufacturers from all around the world were just beginning to grasp the basics of creating alternative-fuel cars. Hybrid vehicles had been experimented with for more than a decade, with Honda and Toyota releasing their contributions in the very late 1990s. Electric vehicles had always been around in one form or another, but rarely made much impact. Indeed, General Motors was deemed to have 'killed the electric car' when it took back and then crushed all its EV1 electric cars and only a few carmakers had built a few token electric vehicles since. Hydrogen had barely got off the ground too – Honda continues to run trials with its FCX Clarity saloon, but the technology forever looks a decade away from viability.

In the early 1990s, Mazda experimented with both hydrogen and electric drive technology – using the MX-5 as a guinea pig. The company had set up a department looking into electric drivetrains and in 1993 it created three prototype electric MX-5s, in conjunction with Japan's Chugoku Electric Power company. As was common for electric cars of the age, performance was lethargic. A bank of sixteen nickel-cadmium batteries sited throughout the vehicle provided enough 'juice' for 179km (111 miles) of range – respectable by modern standards.

Mazda optimistically declared performance to be similar to that of a 1.5-litre, automatic car of the time. However, 25mph (40km/h) could only be reached in 4.2 seconds, partly down to the car's considerable bulk, while the benchmark 0-62mph sprint took 21.5 seconds – more than double that of the petrol car. Its kerb weight of 1410kg (3,109lb) was almost 50 per cent greater than that of the standard, 1.6-litre car. Then, as today, battery weight was very much the enemy of performance in electric cars.

At the time hydrogen appeared a more realistic proposition. Hydrogen vehicles can be refuelled just like a standard petrol car. Rather than explore the fuel-cell route more common nowadays, Mazda's hydrogen MX-5 used a novel rotary engine from the RX-7. Better performing than the electric version at thirteen seconds to 62mph, the hydrogen car was also cleaner than the petrol model. Hydrogen gas was stored in metal hydride powder, which absorbs the cooled, pressurised hydrogen atoms. The car's boot full of aluminium storage canisters was less practical than that of the petrol models, of course, but the benefits of hydrogen lay elsewhere – its use as a fuel produces no global warming-causing carbon dioxide and no cancer-causing hydrocarbons are generated.

Ultimately, neither hydrogen nor electric MX-5s have seen the light of day. Enterprising individuals have produced their own electric-powered MX-5s and others have fitted petrol-fuelled rotary engines for performance, but no official production model has been created. Hydrogen's benefits are no longer as apparent as they were back in the 1990s, either. The gas is extremely energy-consuming to manufacture in any quantity, reducing its environmental credentials before it gets anywhere near the storage tank in a car.

For the foreseeable future, it seems that efficient, low-pollution MX-5s will be created using more traditional means, by improving the standard internal combustion engine, reducing weight and improving aerodynamics.

The MX-5's boot space was compromised further when Mazda built a hydrogen prototype! MAZDA

The electric MX-5 was perhaps ahead of its time. MAZDA

1996 – MAZDA MIATA M COUPÉ

Mazda first explored coupé versions of the MX-5 in 1992. A single prototype was created in the USA, painted in deep metallic blue, but beyond one or two photographs released by the factory, the MX-5 coupé never saw the light of day. Mazda Japan explored the concept once again in 1994 with the less attractive ME 1008 2 – a cut-off tail and faired-in lights took away some of the MX-5's more dainty styling touches.

The company's first serious exploration into an MX-5 Coupé came in 1996, when Mazda USA once again developed a coupé model. Painted in vivid metallic yellow, the Miata M Coupé was a development of the original 1992 concept, but significant work had gone into the model's finish and it was proudly presented at the 1996 New York Auto Show, where press and public alike gave a unanimous thumbs-up.

Even at a glance the car was distinct from a convertible MX-5 with the standard hard top. The front end might have been similar, but aft of the A-pillar the USA design team had made several alterations to balance out the newly installed roof. The roofline itself had distinct echoes of the RX-7, and it blended into a raised boot-line to create a flowing curve from the roof down to the edge of the boot lid. Less obvious at a glance was the Zagato-inspired 'double-bubble' roof profile, a subtle raised hump above both driver and passenger. The rear haunches also seemed more pronounced. Wider, deeper side skirts, 16in alloy wheels with low-profile 205/55 R16 tyres and a wider track gave the car a more powerful stance.

M Coupé, a name later used by BMW, previewed the look of a fixed-roof Mk1 MX-5 that never came. MAZDA

Under the bonnet was the MX-5's standard 1.8-litre engine, tuned slightly to develop 133bhp at 6,500rpm and 155Nm (114lb ft) of torque at 5,500rpm. A yellow-painted cam cover enlivened the under bonnet area. At the back, a carbon fibre-tipped Remus exhaust gave the concept a deeper, louder tone. American magazine *Road & Track* described it as 'providing the sensation of being on the starting grid at Le Mans', when it tested the car in 1996. Performance saw no increase thanks to the concept's heavier kerb weight. To make the one-off vehicle, the roof was constructed from hand-formed fibreglass, rather than a thinner, lighter sheet of steel such as a production car might feature.

The M Coupé's interior was more production ready, however. A suede-like material covered the otherwise standard seats, the old shelf used for roof storage had been converted to a convenient luggage area, and Momo metal pedals were fitted in the footwell. Otherwise it was all standard MX-5.

Car design legend Peter Brock, designer of the Shelby Cobra Daytona Coupé, praised the car's design in *Road & Track*, but criticised the subtlety of the double-bubble roof and the overly large, standard production mirrors. Sadly, production itself was never on the cards, as Tom Matano, at the time executive vice president of Mazda R&D confirmed. 'The Miata M Coupé was purely meant as a styling exercise,' he told the magazine. 'In the spirit of past sports cars that began life as convertibles and were later changed to coupés – cars such as the Triumph GT6 – we wanted to see how the Miata design would lend itself to this new format.' It would be 2004 before Mazda Japan finally created a production MX-5 coupé, and then only in a limited run.

2000 – MAZDA MIATA MONO-POSTO CONCEPT

Each year, the city of Las Vegas, Nevada, plays host to the SEMA Show. The Speciality Equipment Market Association (SEMA) brings together the great and the good of international car builders, tuners and accessory companies, and has grown so large that manufacturers themselves often reserve special vehicles for the show, rather than launching them at international motor shows.

In 2000, Mazda USA displayed the Miata Mono-Posto concept car. While clearly based on the Mk2 MX-5, the

The MX-5 Mono-Posto added a modern twist to a retro racecar look. MAZDA

Mono-Posto harked back to endurance racing cars of the 1950s. Often based on modified road vehicles, these single-seat racers used aerodynamic bodywork to achieve huge speeds on the famous Mulsanne Straight at Le Mans, as well as other international circuits.

With no windscreen and only a single seat, the Mono-Posto concept was immediately evocative of these glorious racecars. Its limited interior consisted of a racing seat, gauges and steering wheel, all supplied by Sparco. Finished in Pearl Red Mica paintwork and featuring a tiny aluminium roll hoop behind the cockpit, it wasn't difficult to imagine the car speeding around a circuit.

To that end, the stock 1.8-litre four-cylinder gained an HKS turbocharger, raising power from 140 to 190hp, and torque more than doubled to 329Nm (243lb ft). An air scoop on the bonnet helped cool the tuned motor, while a single exhaust tip emerged from the centre of the rear bumper. This was surrounded by a silver-painted diffuser-style section, and the rear number plate recess was smoothed over to further bolster the racing image.

Chassis changes included HKS Hiper Damper coilover suspension, which lowered the car over 18x8in and 18x9.5in front and rear three-piece wheels from Racing Hart alloys. These were shod with 225/35 ZR18 and 225/30 ZR18 Pirelli tyres. Stopping power came courtesy of four-wheel Baer cross-drilled disc brakes and four-pot callipers. The styling may have been worthy of the Las Vegas strip, but the Mono-Posto was every inch a racing machine.

2003 – MAZDA IBUKI

By 2003, the motoring press had begun to speculate on the future of the MX-5, anticipating the arrival of an all-new model. That anticipation reached fever pitch when Mazda unveiled the 2003 Ibuki concept. Though not officially branded with the MX-5 tag, the clean, tidy roadster concept could only have been one vehicle. Looking back now, it is clear to see the concept's inspiration on the Mk3

The 2003 Mazda Ibuki Concept was one of the best indications of what a Mk3 MX-5 would look like. MAZDA

MX-5, in particular the treatment of the front lights and the blistered wheel arches.

As with many concepts though, much of the Ibuki never saw production. One of the most striking aspects of the concept was the frameless window – a production impossibility, but a beautiful detail that drew inspiration from old Le Mans racers such as the Lotus XI. The frameless glass continued into the side windows, which curved down more steeply than would be practical for production.

Shorter by 315mm (12.4in) than a production MX-5, the Ibuki was visibly more compact, its proportions exaggerated by huge alloy wheels on run-flat tyres, and incredibly short front and rear overhangs. Small, narrow light fittings evoked the old sidelight fixtures of the original MX-5 and endowed the Ibuki with a front end that survived largely unchanged in style when the third-generation model finally hit the streets.

The interior was far from production reality, however. The centre console stretched not only right throughout the car and dashboard, but under the windscreen

and out onto the bonnet. The controls on the dash were exceedingly simple touch-sensitive arrays. A stubby, symmetrical gearstick and handbrake sat on the centre console between the seats and while the passenger's dashboard was completely bare, the driver enjoyed two pod-like dials behind a sporty three-spoke steering wheel. The whole interior had a satisfyingly industrial feel, helped by wide swathes of metal, rather than slabs of plastic.

Under the bonnet, the Ibuki was much more high-tech than contemporary MX-5s. A 1.6-litre MZR inline-four replaced the existing engines and hinted at the MZR units soon to be dropped into the Mk3 MX-5, while assistance from a hybrid electric motor improved both low-down torque and top-end power. The latter was estimated at 180bhp at 7,500rpm and the 244Nm (180lb ft) torque peak came in at 6,000rpm. Reinforcing the eco credentials of the hybrid set up, the engine could stop when the car was at a standstill, restarting as the driver put the car into gear, ready to move off.

2004 – MAZDA ROADSTER COUPÉ TS CONCEPT

With the MX-5 Coupé being a Japan-only version, Tokyo Motor Show goers were enticed further in 2004 with the appearance of the Roadster Coupé TS Concept. Overtly retro in style, a series of cosmetic modifications turned it from modern coupé into retro racer.

According to Mazda, the car's style was influenced by old European sports cars, specifically those created by Carlo Abarth in the 1960s. Abarth's tiny creations usually clothed humble Fiat mechanicals in wonderful voluptuous bodies. Mazda's TS was not too dissimilar, hiding the standard 1.8-litre engine beneath a bright red paint job and Italianesque white and green stripes.

At the front, a new bumper and headlight arrangement was reminiscent of several 1960s sports cars, with traditional round headlights hooded by Perspex covers. The front bumper also extended further forward, giving the impression of a more aerodynamic shape.

The rear saw similarly retro treatment, each tail light cluster being replaced by a new unit that contained twin, round lights. A small spoiler sat on the boot lid, and the MX-5's usual exhaust system made way for a single pipe slightly offset from the car's centre line.

Another coupé MX-5, the TS took its inspiration from old Italian coach-built sports cars, like those of Carlo Abarth. MAZDA

2009 – MAZDA MX-5 SUPERLIGHT VERSION

Low weight has always been central to the MX-5 experience, so it is only right that this characteristic was honoured, in 2009's 995kg (2,194lb) Superlight Version. Below the car's waistline it could easily be mistaken for any 2009 MX-5 – it shares the same body panels, albeit missing the door handles, and the same flared arches. The light fittings are more distinctive and hint at the car's concept status, but otherwise there is very little to distinguish it from the road car.

That all changes further up. The windscreen was notably absent and where the tonneau cover would normally store the car's folded roof, two sculpted roll hoops protruded from the rear deck. With no need for door seals, a carbon panel encircled the cockpit, blurring the line between interior and exterior, while a tiny rear-view mir-

The MX-5 Superlight Concept was all about simplicity, a light body, a 1.8-litre engine and a basic, no frills cabin, but with exquisite detailing. MAZDA

The MX-5 Superlight Concept – no frills fun all the way. MAZDA

ror peeked from the top of the dashboard. Completing the look, a black-painted aluminium bonnet contrasted sharply with the concept's gleaming white paint.

With no roof, it is the interior became very obvious. Two brown leather bucket seats dominated and the same material wrapped the standard MX-5 steering wheel, the distinctly non-standard dashboard, the centre console, handbrake and gear lever. Ventilation and a radio became irrelevant, given the lack of roof, so the dash featured only a starter button and two aircraft-style toggle switches, one for the fuel pump and the other for the ignition. The dashboard's only concession to luxury was an integrated slot in which to place an iPhone, which can then be used to display additional instruments, or navigation data.

Where normally carpets and sound-deadening material would sit, the tub of the Superlight is simply painted metal, giving it the look of a racecar. Only the standard instruments belie the Superlight's humble origins and in fact, those origins are more humble than might be expected. Instead of the premium MX-5's 2.0-litre MZR engine, the Superlight's engineers based the car on the less potent 1.8, to prove that low weight, rather than increased power, could be an alternative route to higher performance. Tweaked with only a stainless steel air intake and a rasping exhaust system from the Mazda3 MPS, the

Superlight develops only 124hp at 6,500rpm and 167Nm (123lb ft) of torque.

Acceleration is more impressive than those figures suggest, at 8.9 seconds to 100km/h (62mph) and on for an estimated top speed of 209km/h (130mph). The car's low weight also reduces fuel consumption. A combined economy figure of 6.3ltr/100km (44.8mpg) makes it the most fuel-efficient MX-5 to date, despite being one of the most exciting to drive.

Perhaps closest in ethos to 2000's Mono-Posto concept, the Superlight evoked a high-tech feel inside and out, but the thrills it offered were distinctly of an earlier era.

2010 – MAZDA MIATA SUPER 20 CONCEPT

Ten years after the Miata Mono-Posto concept hit the SEMA show, Mazda unveiled another MX-5 concept to celebrate two decades of the seminal roadster. Befitting SEMA's aftermarket ethos, the Super 20 played host to a list of upgraded parts. Central to the concept was the new engine. Based on the regular car's 2.0-litre unit, engine specialists Cosworth reworked the motor and equipped it with a supercharger to boost output.

The chassis was also re-worked, with Mazdaspeed coilovers and a strut tower brace, and Racing Beat hollow anti-roll bars. The car's 16in alloy wheels were sourced from Enkei and Mazda fitted chunky racing tyres. Behind these, upgraded brakes were sourced from StopTech and SpeedSource. Exterior changes continued with the moody dark grey paint, flecked with a gold metallic finish. A black accessory hard top replaced the standard cloth roof and dark, matte-finish stripes lined the lower bodywork and bumpers.

The colour scheme was picked out with orange accents, a colour also featuring on the roll cage and con-trasting stitching inside. A unique exterior touch was the use of tiny metal door handles, sourced from the Mk1 MX-5. Also inspired by the Mk1, the Super 20 lacked the Mazda badge on its nose, instead featuring a small Mazda graphic, offset to the side.

2011 – MAZDA MIATA SPYDER CONCEPT

Mazda showed its Super 20 concept again at the SEMA show in 2011, this time joined by a new, open-top version – the Spyder Concept. Visually it evoked the production Porsche Boxster Spyder, a similarity most noticeable in the lightweight bikini-style half roof, stretched over two rear buttresses.

Painted white and riding on 17in Advan alloy wheels, the Spyder cut a low profile, helped by the less tall. windscreen and reduced ride height. Brushed stainless steel badging completed the exterior changes and Mazdaspeed again provided coilover suspension to improve the car's handling. A 2.0-litre MZR engine also featured, but tuned to run on sustainable isobutanol biofuel. A lightweight lithium-ion battery replaced the usual lead-acid unit.

2012 – MAZDA MX-5 GT CONCEPT

Mazda has rarely endowed the MX-5 with large power fig-ures from the factory, preferring to educate on the virtues of lightweight and simplicity. That changes for many of the company's concept cars though, which increasingly feature power upgrades as well as changes to the styling and spec-ification.

Jota Sport, the Kent-based concern that developed the British GT Championship GT4 MX-5, was drafted in to work on a new high-performance concept, shown at the

The MX-5 GT Concept is not yet in production, but provides a clear look at the potential of the Mk3 MX-5. JOTA SPORT

2012 Goodwood Festival of Speed. Painted in a vivid orange, rather than the racer's metallic green, the GT Concept was nevertheless a road-going racer, with improvements to the engine, suspension and bodywork.

Unlike the racecar, the GT Concept remains naturally aspirated. Power has risen from the 158bhp of the standard 2.0-litre engine, to 205bhp, delivered shortly before a raised 7,800rpm red line. A loud, dual-tipped exhaust completes the mechanical transformation and the car retains the standard six-speed manual gearbox. To improve handling on the track, the springs and dampers were changed, and the ride height dropped by 35mm (1.4in). The interior is largely unchanged from the standard car, with the exception of new Recaro bucket seats, carbon fibre panels on the dashboard and Alcantara gaiters for the gearstick and handbrake.

On the outside, a front splitter and rear lip spoiler, a rear diffuser through which the dual-tip exhaust emerges and matte-black detailing on the wheel arches and side skirts supplement the orange paint. Both wing mirrors and even the Mazda emblem on the nose, have a matt black finish.

As of early 2013, Mazda was still undecided on whether to put the GT Concept into production. A road-going version would cost around £30,000 and while offering more performance than the standard Roadster Coupé, that figure would bring the car uncomfortably close in price to more prestigious rivals.

2012 – MAZDA MX-5 YUSHO PROTOTYPE

A production car in all but production numbers – and not dissimilar to the GT Concept in that respect – the MX-5 Yusho was shown at the 2012 Leipzig Motor Show beside its more production-ready cousin, the Senshu edition. While the Senshu was standard, the Yusho, Japanese for 'Victory', was tuned to highlight the performance potential of the MX-5.

Central to the tuning package was a supercharger conversion from American MX-5 tuning specialist, Flyin' Miata. This was combined with a modified engine management system, new fuel injectors and a high-flow sports catalyst. Cosworth pistons and connecting rods improved durability, and a new exhaust system allowed acoustic control of the exhaust note – not dissimilar to the system found in Ferraris and Aston Martins. Overall, the changes increased power and torque throughout the rev range, raising the 2.0-litre engine's power from 158bhp to 241bhp. That gave the MX-5 enough power to reach 241km/h (150mph), while other changes also improved the car's acceleration.

The car features a standard six-speed manual transmission, upgraded with a sports clutch. A shorter, 4.1:1 final drive ratio shortens the gearing for better acceleration. Suspension has been upgraded all-round – the Yusho uses shortened Eibach springs and Bilstein dampers, with stronger anti-roll bars. The 17x8in anthracite grey alloy wheels are wrapped in a semi-slick Toyo tyre, for maximum track performance. Exterior modifications are limited to a matt-white vinyl wrap, small rear spoiler and carbon fibre-look rear diffuser. The interior features a suede-trimmed steering wheel and Alcantara-covered Recaro sport seats. Visually, the Yusho might not match the drama of some MX-5 concepts, but its production readiness is, for some, even more exciting.

2012 – MAZDA MX-5 SUPER25 CONCEPT

Following on from 2011's Super 20 concepts, the Super25 was developed by Mazdaspeed to hint at an endurance racing variant of the MX-5.

Launched at the 2012 SEMA show in Las Vegas, the Super25's most striking attribute is the four-lamp unit mounted high on its front bumper. It joins a striking red and white paint finish, a hard top, and Volk Racing T37 six-spoke alloy wheels, wrapped in sticky BF Goodrich g-Force tyres.

Inside, the race-prepared specification continues. The single Sparco Evo racing seat has been customised with an unusually named 'ultra-suede' material and perforated red inserts. It also features a Sparco racing harness. A suede-wrapped Sparco R323 steering wheel replaces the regular airbag unit and a data-logger allows the driver to keep an eye on engine parameters during a long race.

The car's number – 55 – has particular significance. It was the number carried by the 1991 Le Mans race-winning 787B, a lucky omen for any endurance racing vehicle.

The Super25 concept was Mazda's idea of an endurance-racing MX-5.
MAZDA

Flyin' Miata

Several companies throughout the world are known for their tuned MX-5s, but Flyin' Miata in the United States has gained a reputation beyond that of many of the others. Set up by Bill and Teri Cardell in 1983, as The Dealer Alternative, the garage specialised in the repair and servicing of prestigious marques like Porsche and Audi.

That all changed one day in 1989, when a customer came in with a brand new Miata and a new business was born. The Dealer Alternative built its first turbocharged Miata within the first few months. In 1996, the business moved to Colorado and began working on Miatas exclusively. The shop began producing unique parts for the Miata, many of which were named under the Flyin' Miata brand and the company changed its name to match in 2000.

While the business develops a range of performance products for the Miata, it is engine tuning and, more specifically, engine conversions for which Flyin' Miata is most famous. Working with Tennessee-based V8 Roadsters, Flyin' Miata can convert a standard 1.6 or 1.8-engined 1989-2005 MX-5 into a V8-powered monster.

Using the popular, light and reliable General Motors LS series engines, Flyin' Miata developed a new tubular subframe and fabricates modifications allowing the V8 to fit into the Miata's engine bay. And fit it does, taking up only a little more space than the four-cylinder units. More impressively, the cars handle almost as well as the original vehicles, despite having more than double the power. Weight increases by little more than 90kg (198lb) and a third of that is over the rear axle, maintaining the MX-5's even weight distribution. The conversion requires no exterior modifications, so few observers would realise the car is different, unless they hear it.

With a minimum of 300bhp and 406Nm (300lb ft) of torque, performance vastly out-punches that of even highly tuned standard four-cylinder MX-5s. Mk2 Miatas are most ripe for conversion, since they offer a larger engine bay and stiffer chassis as standard, but many Mk1 conversions have been carried out. Flyin' Miata is working on a conversion for the Mk3 models. If any proof were needed that the MX-5 can be all things to all people, the ability to slot a V8 engine under the bonnet should be sufficient.

CHAPTER 12

THE MX-5, RE-BODIED

For some, neither production models nor concept vehicles are enough. The MX-5's strong mechanicals and talented chassis – not to mention the ease of bolting on new panels on earlier cars – has made it a popular basis for re-bodied and remodelled versions. If the MX-5's traditional styling is all that is holding you back from your dream sports car, why not turn it into something else entirely?

PIT CREW ROADSTER (JAPAN)

One of the most well-known MX-5 upgrades, the Pit Crew Roadster is heavily inspired by several classic sports cars, including the Ginetta G3, G4 and G12, as well as the classic lines of the Volkswagen Karmann-Ghia.

Based near the Suzuka Grand Prix circuit in Japan, the tiny Pit Crew Racing garage has sold kits worldwide. The greatest difference between the Mk1 MX-5 and the Pit Crew kit is at the front end, where a curved, single-piece bumper, with integrated round headlamps, replaces the regular bumper and pop-up units. Modifications at the rear replace the composite one-piece tail lamps with twin, stacked lights.

Further adding to the retro theme, many owners fit wide, bolt-on arches, a central-exit exhaust at the rear, and furnish their cars with chrome accents. A single, central windscreen wiper is also a popular addition, as are chrome bullet door mirrors.

MEVX5 (UK)

Many re-bodied MX-5s replicate the classic sports car look of older cars, but that isn't the case with the MEVX5. Leicestershire kit-car builder MEV turns the Mk1 MX-5 into a modern day coupé or roadster, with the further option of a lightweight track day car using an entirely new chassis.

Convertible and coupé versions cost £2,650 plus VAT and turn the soft MX-5 lines into a sharp-suited sports car with more than a hint of Lotus Elise inspiration. All the panels bond to the original Mazda bodywork for ease of assembly (which buyers have to install themselves), while a choice of front-end designs and lighting styles lets buyers personalise a little further. The MX-5's standard interior is retained, as is its running gear.

MEV's Superlight is a more thorough re-engineering, using a purpose designed tubular chassis. The windscreen is ditched for a small fly screen and the dashboard is also redesigned. MEV claims that the car is 400kg (882lb) lighter than a standard MX-5, though at £3,895 plus VAT, it isn't as financially accessible. Having a new chassis, the Superlight also requires an Individual Vehicle Approval (IVA) test to be road legal.

RETROFORZA (UK)

Essex-based Retroforza takes its inspiration from the glorious performance cars of the 1950s and 1960s, the influence of which can clearly be seen in its body kit for the Mk1 MX-5. It most closely resembles the classic Ferrari 250 GTO, but has echoes of other Grand Tourers of the age in its elongated form, chrome detailing and voluptuous curves.

The Retroforza is sold in kit form and the company says a full conversion from a standard, road-legal MX-5 can take around 100 hours of work. The body comes as a four-piece unit that can be either bolted or bonded into place. A lighting pack is also supplied. Full kits start from a reasonable £2,395, though in many cases this doubles the cost of the subject car.

The MEVX5 is a lightweight, rebodied MX-5 available as a coupé, convertible or roadster. MEV LTD

SIMPSON DESIGN ITALIA & MANTA RAY (USA)

Similar to the UK's Retroforza kit, the Simpson Design Italia conjures up images of 1960s sports cars, namely the Ferrari 275 GTB. The Italia II line takes that a step further with a more original design, while the Manta Ray pays homage to 1950s' and 1960s' Bertone and Michelotti concept and production cars.

Based out of Clinton, Washington, Simpson Design cre-

ates its products on the frames of Mk1 and Mk2 MX-5s, the latter for the Italia II line of cars. Composite sections replace the main body panels, including the wings, front and rear ends and bonnet. Italia and Italia II conversions even feature a classic style, front-hinged one-piece bonnet. While the kits are relatively expensive, a basic component package costing from US$8,500 and turnkey cars from US$14,900, the work is to an extremely high quality and turns the little MX-5 into one of the most distinctive cars on the road.

Mitsuoka's Himiko is a striking take on a retro-style MX-5 and perhaps one of the most bizarre creations you'll ever see!
BOTH MITSUOKA MOTOR (JAPAN)

MITSUOKA HIMIKO (JAPAN)

Mitsuoka is perhaps most famous for the Viewt. Based on two generations of the humble Nissan Micra hatchback, the Viewt transforms the car into a replica of the MkII

Jaguar, with varying levels of success. Similarly dubious is the Himiko, based on the third-generation MX-5.

Named after an ancient Japanese queen, the Himiko is almost unrecognisable from the MX-5 on which it is based, except for the shape of the doors and the interior,

furnished with Mitsuoka's 'wooden' trim that is unlikely to have come from a tree.

The Himiko also uses the MX-5's windscreen surround and roof designs, both soft top and retractable hardtop. And while the wheelbase is extended to suit the unusual mix of styling cues, the mechanicals are standard MX-5. All Himikos use the 2.0-litre MZR engine, with the option of manual or automatic transmission. The Himiko is hand assembled at the Mitsuoka factory in Toyama City, Japan.

CHAPTER 13

MX-5 MKI BUYING GUIDE

The earliest examples of the MX-5 are now more than twenty years old, but unlike many cars of the era, there is no reason to be put off by that age, even if the car is to be used as a daily vehicle.

Mazda engineered the MX-5 thoroughly and its inherent virtues, including lightweight and simplicity, mean that it is easy on its constituent components. It is not unusual to find MX-5s still using 'consumable' components – that in other cars one would expect to have been replaced during the car's life – that they left the factory with.

That's not to say that buyers should not exercise caution when looking for a car, regardless of whether they intend to restore it as a project, modify it, or simply use it as a characterful and fun daily driver. With thousands of MX-5s still on the road, prospective buyers can afford to be picky and shop around for the model that suits them best.

WHICH MODEL TO CHOOSE?

For those looking at early cars, the choice is fairly simple, even if the waters have been muddied by several years of Japanese imports hitting the market.

Pre-1993, the choice will be among 1.6-litre models only and unless a special edition model is a priority for its extra equipment, the colour choice is likely to be between white, blue and red. The paintwork has proved fairly hardy, even on the earliest cars, although red can suffer from fading, many such vehicles taking on a pinkish hue, unless the body has been well looked after. Red cars are also likely to be the most common, with blue and white becoming rare, and increasingly desirable as a result.

Silver and British Racing Green models are currently the most popular on the used market, the latter as a result

For many MX-5 fans, original and standard is the way to go. ANTONY INGRAM

Eunos imports were once frowned upon, but many now prefer them for their higher equipment levels and reduced likelihood of rust. ANTONY INGRAM

of its classic appearance. Imported V-Spec models, with their tan leather, green paintwork and wooden trim, spend the least time on sale – many say they're the perfect mix of modern and classic. Expect to pay more for these cars.

Post-1993, the 1.8 engine replaced the 1.6. Some drivers prefer the 1.8 for its extra torque and longer final drive ratio, which makes for more relaxed cruising, but others may wish to seek out an early 1.6 for its snappy acceleration and more revvy nature. Post-1995 1.6 models will be of the de-tuned 90bhp version. Drivers unconcerned about performance will find them a worthy choice and relatively inexpensive to insure.

Bodywork

MX-5s may be mechanically sound, but unfortunately they are not immune to rust and many will have succumbed to the curse of iron oxide over the years. There are several areas around the bodywork that need careful inspection. The good news is that the large bonnet isn't one of them, because it is made from aluminium. It may have been peppered with stone chips, however, and is also susceptible to dings and dents, so check it over carefully.

Also ensure that the bonnet lines up evenly with the front wings, since discrepancies could be the result of poor accident repairs – this goes for most shut-lines on the car. While carrying out an inspection, look for other telltale accident signs, like overspray on rubber seals, or evidence of paint runs from poor re-sprays.

It's worth noting that the pop-up headlamp covers rarely lined up perfectly with the bonnet and front bumper and so misalignment isn't necessarily evidence of anything untoward. The front and rear bumpers are incredibly resilient, and can shrug off quite hefty knocks, but check to ensure they have not been dislodged by any low-speed incidents. Budget for replacements if they show any significant dents.

And so to the MX-5's Achilles heel. Mazda galvanised some of its body panels, but not all, meaning that some areas of the bodywork and sills are more susceptible to rust than others. Many MX-5s will have had work on their outer and inner sills by now, as a result of poorly designed drainage for the convertible hood. Small drainage holes are located in each sill, where water from the roof runs down channels and eventually exits through the bottom of the car. Unfortunately, dirt from the roof collects in these holes and combines with road grime to block them. Water from the roof then becomes trapped in the sill area and quickly causes rust.

This often goes unnoticed on the inner sills, but this is a structural area of the car and correct treatment is vital. The proximity of this area to the seatbelt mounting points means an MOT (UK roadworthiness text) failure if rust has taken hold. It can also spread further along the sills and if it is really bad, then the inner sills may need replacing as well as their outer counterparts.

A tell tale sign that water is getting trapped in the sills is a sloshing sound when driving after a rainstorm. It is wise to check the sill areas regularly and clean out the

Check the bodywork for scrapes, dents and uneven panels.
ANTONY INGRAM

drainage holes when necessary to minimise the chances of rust appearing. For peace of mind, it may be worth extending your budget a little to find a car that has had its sills professionally treated.

The front wings are generally fairly rot-free, so if they are getting rusty then the car may have led a hard life. Rust is most likely to appear on the leading edge of the wing, where it meets the large plastic bumper. The same applies to any rust under the bonnet, but if there is rust in the boot, the battery tray, located behind the boot trim inside the offside front wing, needs checking. The MX-5 requires a special gel battery and using a cheaper one with a liquid electrolyte can result in leaks, which corrode the metal below.

Buyers wanting to buy a corrosion-free car have got two primary options. One is to buy the best UK car they can afford, since many of the pricier examples have led pampered, garaged lives, and will usually look immaculate. The other is to seek out a Japanese import, since the Japanese authorities don't salt roads in winter, eliminating the brine sludge that quickly eats into vulnerable bodywork.

Japanese cars certainly aren't immune to rust and, indeed, some may be more susceptible since they lack the underseal of UK cars, but since many of them spent the first decade of their lives on Japanese roads, they have a

Chrome-ringed vents are non-standard, but they're a cheap and easy way to brighten up the interior. ANTONY INGRAM

It's getting more difficult to find a standard MX-5, but this V-Spec has avoided too many aftermarket touches.
ANTONY INGRAM

A rear spoiler was an option on V-Spec models. ANTONY INGRAM

head start on UK cars. The import date needs to be checked, because the less time a car has spent in the UK, the less likely it is to have suffered rust.

Visually, the easiest way to distinguish whether you're looking at a Japanese car or a UK example is the badge – imports usually have 'Eunos Roadster' badging. Otherwise, check the rear number plate recess – it is square on imports and rectangular on UK cars. Japanese models also feature a centrally mounted rear brake light.

Hoods

Mazda did a thorough job on the MX-5's hood, and though a car may well have had a replacement in its twenty-odd years of life, it should still offer all the qualities of the original – a watertight fit, relatively low noise on the move and a double skin to the rear.

Ideally, you should be able to see out of the rear screen, though fogging of the plastic is a common ailment, resulting from the window being constantly folded and un-folded with the roof. Drivers can prevent this by un-zipping

Hoods vary widely in quality and condition, and some are more expensive to replace than others. ANTONY INGRAM

MX-5 interiors are simple and robust, but ensure everything works. ANTONY INGRAM

Make sure interiors have all the right equipment, especially on models like this V-Special. ANTONY INGRAM

the rear screen before lowering the roof, but since this is a little less convenient than flicking the hood back in one move, few bother.

A rear screen with a split down the middle could be the result of it having been opened in very cold weather. The plastic becomes brittle in the cold and snaps rather than folds when the roof is dropped. Unfortunately, it can't be replaced separately, so if a hood with a split rear screen means an entirely new roof. If the rear screen has split or is simply very fogged, the chances are that the hood may be up for replacement anyway and is likely suffering in other areas. Splits in the stitching around the windows are common, as are splits in the vinyl around the rear rain gutter.

If a car has had a hood replacement at some stage, its quality can be assessed according to whether there is a line of stitching a few inches out from the rear window's edge. If there is, it is a single-skin hood and not the double-skinned version the MX-5 was sold with. Higher quality replacements are double skinned at the rear and if the previous owner has really spent some money on the hood, it will likely use mohair fabric rather than the original vinyl. Mohair has a more pleasant appearance and feel, and folds more easily in cold weather than the heat-sensitive vinyl. Some aftermarket hoods also came with glass screens to eliminate the fogging problem and some of those may even be heated.

Hood replacement can be costly and even more so if labour rates are taken into account. A new vinyl hood with PVC rear window starts at around £200. Mohair and PVC units can be double that, while a vinyl hood with an upgraded glass rear screen can cost a little under £400 and a mohair hood with a glass window – the most desirable combination – is almost £600.

Check inside the car for leaks. These are most likely to originate from blockages in the rain gutter at the rear of the hood (leading to dampness on the rear shelf), or poor sealing of the rubber around the side windows, which can lead to water dripping onto the seats and carpets. Leaks are not usually serious and should not lead to rust issues, but they are worth addressing to prevent the interior smelling of dampness.

Interior

An MX-5's interior is a simple place, so you won't have to spend too long searching for issues. The potential number of problems is limited, but there are a few common ail-

Some options, such as this Nardi steering wheel, are very desirable.
ANTONY INGRAM

ments to look for. Most common of all are slow electric windows. There can be several causes for this, but the two most frequent faults relate to the electric window motor itself and the cables used to raise and lower the windows. The latter often cause failure of the former – the cables become stiff with age and as they do so, it becomes harder for the motor to lower or raise the glass. If the cables seize, the motor can burn out and then both units need replacing. Best practice is to change or lubricate the cables as a precaution, before the motor fails. If the windows don't work at all, then the motors may already have failed, or it could be as simple as a broken switch.

Another common ailment on older MX-5s is a wobbling speedometer needle, cured by a replacement speedo cable. If the car being inspected has air conditioning, ensure that it works. Many MX-5 buyers are sceptical of the reliability of the pop-up headlights – possibly as a result of owning an old British car with failing electrics or weak vacuum operation – but on MX-5s problems are incredibly rare. Headlamp motors almost never fail, and if the headlights fail to rise, the problem is more likely related to the switch. The units should rise, both with the switch on the steering column stalk and the button below the hazard warning light switch on the dash.

The 1.6-litre, twin-cam 'four' may not be powerful, but it has plenty of character. ANTONY INGRAM

Engine

By and large, there is very little to worry about with regard to the MX-5's engine. It was built to withstand the high pressures of turbocharged combustion in the 323 and without the turbocharger it is an incredibly under-stressed unit that can handle huge mileage with few issues. It's not unknown for cars to top 200,000 miles (321869km), and well looked after examples will still be performing strongly at that mileage.

As a result, buyers should mainly look for common engine maladies and ensure that the unit has been well serviced. The oil level on the dipstick should be checked, while a milky white substance on the underside of the oil filler cap implies a failing head gasket, though this is quite rare. Oil seepage around the cam cover gasket is a common issue, but doesn't result in any major problems and is easily and cheaply fixed.

Many MX-5s have been modified, so a quick check to see if this is the case is always wise. The most obvious and most common modification is an aftermarket cone air filter on the right of the engine bay, replacing the standard airbox. Experts are divided on whether this really improves performance, but indicates that the car may have been driven a little harder than average.

The engine should fire up quickly with a turn of the key and settle into a smooth, if relatively high idle. Listen out for a 'tappety' noise from the cam cover – it is fairly common and not any major cause for concern, but indicates that the hydraulic tappets may need a little adjustment. Usually, it is even simpler than this and an oil flush to clear blocked pathways will typically clear the tappet noise.

With the engine warm, idle speed will drop and oil pressure should fall from around 60psi to 30psi – it can be read on the small central dial at the top of the instrument cluster. Any hunting, stuttering or stalling indicates that the injectors are clogged. Several companies sell sprays that can solve this problem.

Check the car's history or ask the previous owner when the cam belt was last changed. Mazda recommends a change every 54,000 miles, but unlike many cars, breakage doesn't spell disaster for the engine. It is a non-interference unit, which means that if the belt snaps, the pistons and valves do not have an expensive coming together. Even so, it's best to ensure the belt is healthy, and if it is changed, it makes sense to replace the water pump at the same time.

On very rare occasions, early 1.6 cars suffer engine failure as a result of a stretched bolt on the crankshaft pulley. The number of slots identifies early crankshaft pulleys – there are four on early examples, eight on later ones. If a bolt was over-tightened to a later torque figure during a cam belt change, it can stretch and the pulley can wobble, damaging the nose of the crankshaft. Luckily, it is easy to check for – excessive wobble on the pulley indicates damage, as does a lack of power at lower revs, a result of cam and ignition timing going out of sync. If caught early it can be fixed, but if there is excessive play in the pulley a new engine may be required.

Transmission

Like the engine, the MX-5's transmission is largely bulletproof with the correct maintenance. If all is in correct working order, the gearshift should be short, quick and accurate, with every gear engaging cleanly. Don't be too perturbed by a slightly difficult change into first when cold, since the gearbox becomes much slicker as it warms up. Reverse doesn't like to be rushed either, so leave a second or two between selecting forward and reverse gears.

If you have difficulty changing gear there are a few possible explanations. One is that the gear lever linkage oil reservoir has run dry, usually as a result of the rubber seals in the linkage splitting. It calls for an easy do-it-yourself fix, which involves removing the centre console to access the rubber boots, replacing them and then adding a squirt of gearbox oil to the linkages.

A common gear selection problem is caused by failure of the clutch slave cylinder. The unit is mounted to the outside of the gearbox bell housing, right in the line of fire for road grime, water, dirt, rocks and anything else on the road. Eventually the rubber seals perish and each pump of the clutch

then sends fluid out onto the floor, rather than through the hydraulic pipes. The clutch gradually stops working and eventually gear selection becomes impossible.

Checking below the car for a little pool of hydraulic fluid just off-centre from the gearbox is an easy way to spot the problem early. Another is to turn the wheels fully to the left and shine a torch through the gap between wheel and arch onto the driver's side of the gearbox. If the slave cylinder is surrounded by gunk, there's a fair chance it's in need of replacement. The parts are cheap – £15-£20 for a slave cylinder on its own – but access can be tricky for the home mechanic. Parts and labour at a specialist come to around £80. If you've tackled both these jobs and you are still having difficulties changing gear, it could be a sign that the clutch is reaching the end of its life.

The rear differential varies depending on the model. UK 1.6 cars have an open rear differential, while 1.6 Eunos imports use a viscous limited-slip differential and all 1.8 cars have a more sturdy torsen (torque-sensing) limited-slip 'diff'. These are all fairly reliable, though early viscous differentials will likely be losing their limited-slip capabilities and behave more like the basic open diff.

Suspension, Wheels, Tyres and Brakes

From launch the MX-5 was supplied with seven-spoke 14in 'daisies', a wheel design echoing the Minilite-style wheels popular on British sports cars through the 1960s. These were wrapped in 185/65 R14 tyres. The combination sounds wholly inadequate by modern standards, but many pundits believe that the original wheels and tyres are best suited to the bumps of British roads and allow the car to slide around a bit more. Replacement tyres are also incredibly cheap in this size, even as high performance tyres from well-known brands. The original 'daisies' may be looking a little second-hand though and for buyers wanting to keep the car original, plenty of companies offer alloy wheel refurbishment services to bring them back to as-new condition.

Another popular wheel and tyre combination, often used on the second-generation cars and therefore an easy swap, is to fit 15x6.5in alloys and 195/55 R15 tyres. This keeps the rolling radius very similar to the original wheels, but provides a little more grip and traction, though ride quality suffers a little.

Elegant and simple, the MX-5's silhouette has remained similar through each generation. ANTONY INGRAM

Be wary of MX-5s fitted with wheels any larger than 15in. Not only does the ride deteriorate further, highlighting some of the car's natural structural wobbles, but handling and steering-feel also suffer, thanks to the increased unsprung weight. Anything larger than the standard rolling radius also increases the gearing, which degrades acceleration.

The MX-5's standard brakes work fairly well and the car's low weight means discs and pads should last a surprisingly long time, assuming the car isn't driven very hard.

The setup is mostly trouble-free, but older models may suffer from binding callipers. This causes extra resistance and scuffing noises while driving, as well as vibrations through the brake pedal. Left unchecked, the discs and pads can get very hot, causing unpleasant vibrations through the car, so check that the brakes function correctly on any test drive. Make sure the discs and pads still have some life left too. If the discs look overly corroded or have a lip around their edges, they are in need of replacement.

The MX-5's rear lights bore a similarity to those on the Lotus Elan.
ANTONY INGRAM

MX-5s are very reliable, but their paintwork can fade after years in the sun. ANTONY INGRAM

Like most mechanical aspects of the MX-5, the suspension is largely trouble free. One of the most cost-effective ways of making an MX-5 drive better is to have the car four-wheel laser aligned, restoring it to factory setup. This instantly brings out the best in the car and typically costs under £100. Suspension arms can bend on rare occasions, if they've been put under particular punishment, and if a garage is struggling to align the car, this might be the issue.

Several companies sell aftermarket suspension and steering system bush kits for the MX-5. While the quality of these products is high, few recommend them for the MX-5. The extra stiffness can send undesirable bumps through the car and on the road the benefit is fairly small, given the £200-£300 parts and labour cost.

Overall

There is much to recommend the Mk1 MX-5 and for enthusiasts, the 'original is best' mantra still rings true. A good MX-5 will provide years of reliable fun, while costing very little to buy and run. Special editions abound and many offer that extra dose of luxury that may be appreciated in daily driving, but a simple, original car will be perfect for weekend blasts. Provided the car you inspect doesn't hold too many rust issues, the Mk1 MX-5 could be one of the wisest used vehicle purchases on the market.

CHAPTER 14

MX-5 MK2 BUYING GUIDE

It may be no surprise to discover that with so many similarities to the Mk1 MX-5, Mk2 models suffer from the same ailments. However, that also means that they enjoy the same benefits and any buyer experienced in early MX-5s should be able to make important checks without worrying about missing any significant areas.

WHICH MODEL TO CHOOSE?

As a rule, Mk2 MX-5s came with high specifications, particularly on special edition models. Their relative youth next to original MX-5s also means there's a greater choice of cars on the market, so buyers really can afford to be picky. There's little excuse to settle for a poorly maintained car with so many good examples available and the prospective buyer may even find the very latest examples on main dealer forecourts, for extra peace of mind.

Engine choice is between 1.6 and 1.8 litres. The 1.6 models generally have a lower specification, with five-speed rather than six-speed gearboxes and an open rear differential, whereas many 1.8s have a limited-slip unit. They also tend to have lower equipment counts and avoid some of the luxuries of many 1.8 models – air conditioning in particular. Basic 1.8s lack some of that equipment, but generally the later the model, the better specified it will be.

With so many Mk2 models to choose from, buyers can afford to be picky. MAZDA

Wood and leather are desirable on Mk2s, so make sure they're in good condition. MAZDA

Clean, standard MX-5s are nice cars, but special editions will always be a little more popular. MAZDA

Special edition cars are very popular, though some command a higher price than others. The 10th Anniversary models are highly sought-after, as are cars with wood and leather-lined cabins. Buyers shouldn't pay over the odds for a car in poor condition, but it is worth remembering that like-for-like, some of the more unusual models may cost a little more.

It is uncommon to find imported Mk2 models on the used market. Plentiful supply and strong equipment lists on UK-market models – air conditioning, leather trim and unique alloy wheels are all common – meant that fewer buyers were interested in buying overseas models. One may turn up now and then, but in general most cars you'll find will have spent their lives in the UK.

The lack of imported Mk2 models and the car's unavailability with an automatic transmission on the UK market also means that auto cars are very rare. A buyer hankering after an automatic version may have to strike the Mk2 off their search list and look for a Mk1 or Mk3 car, unless they're very lucky. Mk2 automatics do exist, but recent exchange rate differences between the UK and Japan also make them uneconomical to import.

Bodywork

Like the Mk1 cars, rust can be a major issue on Mk2 MX-5s. In fact, some specialists suggest that Mk2 models are even worse, given that they often feature similarly poor bodywork despite their comparative youth. Enthusiasts suggest that Mazda's quality control slipped with early Mk2 models, but the bottom line is that unless the car has been fastidiously maintained, rust could well be taking hold inside the sills.

The cause is identical to that of the Mk1. Water runs down the outside of the roof and through drainage channels. These may keep water out of the cabin effectively, but the tiny exit holes on the sills become clogged by debris. Once this happens the water has nowhere to drain and sits inside the sills, quickly causing rust.

While buyers should usually avoid examining cars in the rain, it may be worth breaking this rule with MX-5s, to listen for the sloshing of water in the sills under braking. This is usually a good sign that the drainage holes have become blocked and the sills may already be at risk.

To replace, the parts for an inner sill alone come to around £200 and buyers taking on a rusty project should

budget for a great deal more, to take labour and other panels into account. It's highly recommended to see an MX-5 specialist for this work, since they will take the time and effort to properly protect the inner sills with wax, reducing the probability that rust will take hold in the future. The worst rust can often be found on cars with aftermarket body kits, which were popular during a certain phase in the MX-5's life. These often held moisture close to already-corroding bodywork, accelerating the rusting process.

Bonnets are again aluminium, so paint chips are the only concern. Front wings are not particularly susceptible to rust, but those that are can be replaced with relative ease, since the panels bolt on. A new front wing costs £140 direct from Mazda. The only other rusty area you are likely to find is on the boot lid. Mk1s don't suffer from this problem but some Mk2s do. Poor drainage can lead to water collecting in the trailing edge of the boot lid, encouraging rust.

Beyond this, check to ensure the panels are free of kinks, that door, boot and bonnet shut-lines are uniform in size, and that there is no evidence of overspray on doors and under the bonnet; these are all signs that the car may have been involved in an accident.

Hoods

As on the Mk1, hoods should generally be in fairly good condition. The hoods were well designed to begin with, so don't typically leak and by the time the Mk2 hit the streets, Mazda had improved quality further. Most Mk2s are likely to feature a glass rear window, which eliminates the 'fogging' problems of the early plastic windows, and many will have a quality mohair hood that is not as likely to split as a cheaper vinyl hood.

This pushes up replacement costs however, so ensure that the car has a decent hood to start with. Budget up to £400 for parts alone on a vinyl hood with a glass rear window and almost £600 for a mohair hood with glass window. Fitting is a laborious process, but one which can be done by the home mechanic to save money on professional fitting.

Cars with factory or aftermarket hard tops can be very desirable and buyers likely to want a hardtop at some stage are well advised to purchase a model with one included. Cars with hard tops go for a premium, but it is still considerably cheaper than buying a brand new top – a genuine, brand new Mazda roof can cost around £1,000. It is also possible to find used hard tops in classified ads and on internet auction sites. These sell for between £250 and £750 depending on condition and colour. Best of all, hard tops from Mk1 vehicles will fit Mk2 cars, and vice-versa.

Interior

MX-5 interiors are robust and hard wearing and, thanks to the large plastic mouldings used on Mk2 models, trim damage is not as likely as it is on Mk1s. At the same time, ensure that the trim is all present and correct. On special edition cars in particular, replacement parts are becoming more difficult to find as the numbers of these models dwindle. If a car is supposed to have a wooden gear knob, for example, ensure that it hasn't been replaced with an aftermarket part.

Seats also need to be in good condition, with no rips or tears. On cloth seats this is less of an issue, albeit unsightly, but leather trim is more expensive and more difficult to replace. It is possible to find second hand units on internet auction sites or from specialists, but the alternative is to pay for a re-trim, which typically costs around £150 per seat.

Later MX-5s tend to be heavily specified with electrical equipment like air conditioning, electric and heated mirrors, heated seats and more. While inspecting a car, ensure all this equipment works as it should. Another common ailment the Mk2 shares with its Mk1 predecessor is that of slow-moving electric windows. Often caused by the cable used to raise and lower the glass, this can eventually seize and burn out the electric motor. A new motor costs up to £130 and a full kit up to £250. If the problem is with the switch, a replacement unit can cost around £50 brand new.

Engine

Engines are typically bombproof. Like earlier cars, Mk2 MX-5s can be driven huge distances, and while they can be intolerant of poor maintenance, any well-maintained car should be absolutely fine, even with a large figure on the odometer. Even cars with high mileage should not use

The MX-5's interior is hardwearing, but ensure everything works as it should. MAZDA

MX-5 engines are almost bulletproof, but need regular maintenance. MAZDA

much oil between checks.

Mk2.5 cars used a later on-board diagnostic system, which makes it even easier for garages to identify any potential problems and renders servicing an easier and quicker process. Even so, the added complication of Mk2 models over their Mk1 counterparts means that the electrics are not quite as robust as on the earlier models. Coil packs are prone to failure in Mk2s and replacing one will cost around £300.

Those later engines should be no less reliable than earlier units, despite added complication from technology like variable valve timing. MX-5 engines need correct maintenance, however, so ensure that any prospective purchase has had regular oil changes and sufficient servicing. Vehicles with a full service history are more desirable and with later Mk2.5 cars in particular, many may still be serviced at Mazda dealerships. Mk2 models have serv-

Mk2.5 MX-5s generally featured larger wheels than previous models. MAZDA

ice intervals every 9,000-12,000 miles or every twelve months, though some enthusiastic owners may service their cars more frequently for even better longevity – 6,000 miles is recommended. If the owner can produce a large folder of bills and service items, then you are probably looking at a well loved car.

Transmission

Transmission issues are as uncommon as they are on earlier MX-5s, even with the six-speed manual found on higher-spec or later Mk2s. On the test drive, you may initially find the gearshift to be a little obstructive, but once the oil has warmed up, the shift should be as quick and slick as the road test reports suggest.

Ailments are not frequent, but most transmission problems are the result of either a failed clutch slave cylinder or the gear linkage oil reservoir running dry. The latter is a simple home fix, as it is on the Mk1. Clutch slave cylinder failures occur for all the same reasons as on the Mk1 too. If you have the skills and equipment, replacement is a fairly simple process and the cylinder itself costs little over £15. To have the work done by a garage, budget another £50 for labour.

Suspension, Wheels, Tyres and Brakes

As with the Mk1 MX-5, Mk2 models are said to handle best on the same diameter wheels they were equipped with from the factory. On early models this was usually 15in, and on later cars, particularly Mk2.5 models, 16in wheels became more common. Any larger than this and the car's delicate ride and handling balance can be negatively affected, with ride quality in particular becoming uncomfortably firm on broken British roads.

Like all MX-5s, the Mk2 also benefits from the fitting of quality tyres. If the car you're inspecting is wearing a no-name brand, it may be a sign that the previous owner has skimped on maintenance costs elsewhere too. And as always, one of the best things you can do to any MX-5 is to have the car fully laser aligned and reset to factory settings. For improving handling, grip, stability and braking, it is the first port of call for many owners. Any car with uprated suspension should also have been professionally aligned after the modification was done.

Suspension components are as resilient as on any other MX-5. Bushes last well, and should not require replacement more frequently than every 60,000 miles and springs and dampers should last even longer, often as long as 100,000 miles – though check to ensure none of the springs have cracked. Many recommend against upgrading suspension bushes unless you plan to drive regularly on-track – ride quality can suffer and for road driving; the benefits don't justify the expense.

Overall

For many, the Mk2 currently represents the best ownership compromise for MX-5 buyers on a budget. Cheaper than the Mk3, but more comfortable and no less reliable than the Mk1, their ubiquity is not difficult to understand. As with the Mk1, however, it is vital that used cars are fully inspected to ensure that a time consuming and expensive repair is not required. Buy the best example you can afford and inspect it thoroughly before the test drive.

CHAPTER 15

MX-5 MK3 BUYING GUIDE

Veterans of car buying say that there is no such thing as a risk-free used car, but a Mk3 MX-5 is about as close to risk free as you can get. Even so, there are still things a prospective purchaser should inspect before buying, to ensure that they get the best possible experience from the latest incarnation of Mazda's roadster.

WHICH MODEL TO CHOOSE?

In common with earlier MX-5s, buyers will find a bewildering degree of choice when shopping for used Mk3s. There's something for almost every budget and with Mk3 MX-5s still on sale brand new, many under a few years old

may still be under a full Mazda warranty, for added peace of mind.

Budget permitting, the main choice is likely to be between the pre- and post-facelift cars. Mazda exercised many subtle changes when the 'Mk3.5' was released, so as well as the more modern styling, later cars are said to handle a little better and higher quality materials are used on the interior. Others may prefer the earlier cars for their simpler, more traditional styling and of course, their lower price tags.

Two engines are available, 1.8 and 2.0-litre MZR four-cylinder units. The former costs less to insure and offers slightly better fuel economy, while remaining fun to drive. The latter is equipped with a six-speed gearbox, reaches

Pick a good Mk3 and it will give you tens of thousands of miles of trouble-free fun. ANTONY INGRAM

160

ABOVE AND BELOW: *Mk3 MX-5s should still be resisting rust, but it's worth ensuring that the hood is still in good condition.* MAZDA (BOTH)

60mph from rest a couple of seconds sooner and many are equipped with performance features like uprated Bilstein dampers and a limited-slip differential. The 2.0-litre models can also be found with a six-speed automatic transmission, with steering wheel-mounted manual shift paddles. Performance is still sprightly and the car may suit those who prefer to cruise, rather than attack bends.

Beyond all the options listed above, Mk3 buyers also have the choice of either traditional, manual soft top, or automatic retractable hardtop. Soft tops are cheaper and lighter, while the hard top offers added safety and security benefits, better noise insulation and the ease of use inherent in pressing a button to raise or lower the roof.

Finally, there will be a wealth of special edition models on the market, all of which offer luxuries and unique touches less likely to be found in standard models. Leather trim, coloured dashboard inserts and metallic paint are all common features of the special editions.

Bodywork

Early MX-5s may be suffering from rust by now, but most Mk3s are still under their original corrosion warranties. Buyers can check with their local Mazda dealership as to whether the warranty is still valid, ensuring the vehicle has had annual check-ups at a Mazda dealer. Even so, any visible signs of rust should be treated with suspicion – they are likely to point towards poorly repaired accident damage. Uneven panel gaps, ill-fitting bumpers front and rear, and mismatched paintwork are indicative of a car that has suffered damage.

There is an exception to the above. The system for drainage on Mk3 MX-5s is near identical to that of earlier cars. Water still runs down off the hood, through drainage channels and out through small holes in the sills. These holes block and lead to water entering the cabin. While this is currently an irritation for some owners, specialists suggest that it could eventually lead to exactly the same rusty sills issue seen on the first two generations of car. For this reason, buyers should carefully check that any prospective purchase has avoided water ingress. The alternative is to seek out the hard-topped Roadster Coupé models, on which water runs off the outside of the roof and down the bodywork, rather than through drainage channels.

Otherwise, most Mk3 MX-5s should be structurally and visually sound. This reduces bodywork inspection to the

usual checks – looking for stone chips in the paintwork, ensuring the sides are free of car parking dents and scrapes, and making sure the large plastic bumpers are not dented from parking damage.

Hoods

Checks here will vary depending on the model being inspected. Soft hoods fit even better than their counterparts in earlier MX-5s and even the earliest cars, built in 2006, should have undamaged soft tops showing very little wear. The tight fit means that leaks from the roof itself should not be an issue and the top will even withstand pressure washing without letting more than a couple of drops into the cabin.

The retractable hard top is equally close fitting and even less likely to let in water. Check when buying to make sure the mechanism works as it should – unlatch and pull the handle on the roof, then press the button to lower it. Once the roof has lowered, press the other button to raise it again, then re-latch it once it settles into position. The whole operation should be free of creaking and sticking. Owners are reporting very few problems with the hard top in terms of operation, so most hard tops should be working as they were when they left Hiroshima.

Interior

There is little to find fault with inside the Mk3's cabin. Rattling and broken trim is uncommon, and all equipment should still be working correctly. Higher-mileage cars may be starting to show some wear on the driver's seat, but not to the same extent as earlier MX-5s.

Post-facelift cars used slightly better quality trim materials and a few different interior mouldings. Notably, the door cup holders on later cars are better integrated into the door moulding, making them less likely to rub against the legs of taller drivers.

Finally, though roofs are generally leak-free, it isn't unknown for leaves or dirt to clog the roof drainage tubes. When this happens, water that would otherwise drain to the ground has nowhere else to go and can find its way inside the cabin. This results in wet carpets and a £400 fix if they are badly damaged by water, so prospective buyers should inspect the carpets for signs of dampness.

The Mk3's hood is as simple as that on previous cars, but should be even more watertight. ANTONY INGRAM

Interiors are often well specified. ANTONY INGRAM

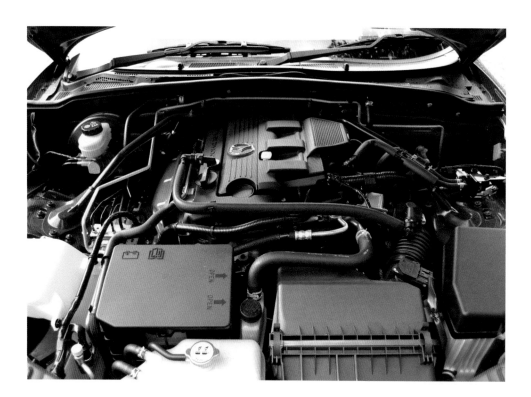

*Both Mk3 engines, the 1.8 and
2.0, are reliable, strong and
relish being worked hard.*
ANTONY INGRAM

Engine

The MX-5's 1.8 and 2.0-litre MZR four-cylinder engines are incredibly reliable. With a lightweight body to push along and developing less power than some contemporaries, both engines are under-stressed and unlikely to develop problems, even at higher mileages.

Features like iron cylinder liners and chain-driven camshafts reduce engine wear and maintenance requirements. There have been some problems reported with variable valve timing mechanisms, which can fail after four years or 54,000 miles – but these are not widely reported, making them very much the exception rather than the rule.

Even harder-driven cars are unlikely to use much oil – there are stories of MX-5s used in racing that don't use a drop of oil all weekend. Buyers should still ask for confirmation of a full service history though, to ensure the car has been looked after throughout its previous tenure. Services should have been carried out annually, or 12,500 miles. The 62,500-mile service involves a spark plug change, but servicing prices for the MX-5 are relatively low. This ensures they are not expensive to maintain, which in turn means that most will have had all the required maintenance.

Transmission

Mk3 MX-5s come with five-speed manual, six-speed manual, or six-speed automatic transmission. Both manuals should have short, precise shift actions and a slick feel. However, they do take a little time to warm up, particularly in colder climates, and they can initially seem notchy and difficult to shift. Ensure test drives allow the gearbox enough time to warm up, as these cold-weather symptoms shouldn't persist. Six-speed manual gearboxes are occasionally known to jump out of third or fourth gear when cold, a problem cured by replacing the baulk rings.

Automatics are also unlikely to cause problems and even owners on notoriously vocal internet forums aren't reporting any issues. Whether in the full automatic mode or using the gearshift paddles on the steering wheel, changes should be smooth and quick, with no jerks or thumps.

Suspension, Wheels, Tyres and Brakes

Tyre wear should not be a major issue on Mk3 MX-5s, with rear tyres lasting up to eighteen months and front tyres managing twice that, though both of these figures

Alloy wheels are standard on all but the most basic Mk3s.
ANTONY INGRAM

can fluctuate subject to how hard the car is being driven. Owners recommend fitting quality brand tyres to make the most of the car's handling characteristics, but with factory wheels no bigger than 17in in diameter, even performance tyres can be relatively inexpensive – less than for many normal family cars.

Very early, base-model Mk3s were fitted with 16in steel wheels, but every other Mk3 used either 16 or 17in alloy wheels, which are vastly more desirable on the used market. The 17in wheels became the norm on special edition cars and any post-facelift MX-5, so virtually all standard Mk3.5 cars will have 17in alloys. These can be prone to kerbing damage however, particularly in cars used regularly for city driving. A car with scraped wheels may also be misaligned. Just as with earlier MX-5s, an alignment is one of the cheapest and simplest ways to improve the handling of your MX-5. This is particularly important with modified cars.

Brakes have caused no problems so far and wear isn't much of an issue given the MX-5's relatively lightweight body. Simple visual checks should confirm how much life the discs and pads have left. Likewise, suspension on Mk3s is fairly trouble free. Some early cars may still have the fairly high ride-height and spring and damper setups crit-

icised in the original press reports. Drivers intending to use the car in a fairly enthusiastic manner may wish to seek out the later cars with improved suspension settings, while the 2.0-litre models also gained Bilstein dampers for improved control.

Overall

The Mk3 could be considered too new to have suffered any major issues yet, but there could be a cloud hanging over its resistance to rust. Those (currently hypothetical) issues aside, the Mk3 and Mk3.5 MX-5s are equally as shrewd an investment as earlier cars.

Depreciation is still yet to fully take its toll, but the Mk3's inherent reliability should ensure it gains the same cult status as its older counterparts. Prospective purchasers – both used and brand new – will no doubt be heartened to learn that the MX-5 was even named Britain's most reliable car by What Car? magazine in August 2012 and, better still, the car with the lowest repair costs. No longer does owning a sports car mean having to pay a premium.

CHAPTER 16

MX-5 IN MOTORSPORT

Several companies make grandiose claims about how many of their sporting models are raced around the world, but few can claim to offer such an affordable way into competitive motorsport as Mazda. To this day, all generations of MX-5 are raced in series across the globe, with many more competing in time trials, hill climbs, autocross, drifting and even simple track days. They might not be raced in the sheer numbers of Caterhams or Porsche 911s, but in terms of accessibility, the MX-5 is hard to beat.

SPEC MIATA (USA)

In 2006, the Sports Car Club of America (SCCA) launched the Spec Miata series. Probably the most well known of all competitive MX-5 racing events, the series was aimed at providing budding racecar drivers with an inexpensive series in which to hone their skills, but an emphasis has always been placed on fun too. Rigid specification rules ensure that the cars are as evenly matched as possible, leaving the competitive element up to the drivers themselves. Like the similar MaX5 series in the UK, Spec Miata was designed to replicate the original Spec Miata series run by Mazda between 1990 and 1991, soon after the car was launched.

The Spec Miata series is divided into several classes, depending on the type of car being used. The SCCA approves three generations of Miata – 1990-1993 cars with 1.6-litre engines, 1994-1997 cars with the 1.8-litre engine and Mk2 Miatas built between 1999 and 2005, with 1.8-litre engines. As of January 2012, 1.6-litre cars were required to weigh 2,330lb (1057kg), Mk1 1.8s ran at 2,350lb (1066kg) and the more powerful Mk2 cars at 2,399lb (1088kg).

The 1.6-litre cars are also allowed to run a modified airbox to improve power, while the 1.8-litre cars are restricted to a standard air intake and throttle restrictor. All cars run on 15x7in alloy wheels with a specified minimum weight and the series specifies a control tyre, a 205/55 R15 made by Hoosier. All cars run Bilstein coilover adjustable suspension with Eibach springs and adjustable sway bars, and steel-braided brake lines.

PLAYBOY MX-5 CUP (USA)

With no class for Mk3 MX-5s in America's popular Spec Miata series, the Playboy MX-5 Cup offers the same level of competitive racing in identical cars, on an even more professional stage. Once again run by the Sports Car Club of America, the Playboy-sponsored MX-5 Cup is described as the entry level of production car-based competition in SCCA Pro Racing – a competitive level that includes single-seater racing, the Trans Am road racing series, and the Pirelli World Challenge. That puts the Cup on an international stage and brings some series racing series within reach of the drivers – not that the racing in the MX-5 Cup itself is not serious.

As with other MX-5 series, car specification is controlled by the organisers. MX-5s built between 2006 and 2012 are eligible for competition, all of 2.0-litre capacity. Engine modifications are limited, consisting of a Mazdaspeed cold air intake system, revised ignition wires and spark plugs, and a modified clutch disc and pressure plate. Power output is around 200bhp.

Mazdaspeed has developed a special suspension package that must be fitted to all cars and suspension alignment and ride height is free. Wheels are stock production items in 17x7in size and the series-spec tyre is a 225/45 R17 made by BF Goodrich. Unlike Spec Miata, hard tops are not permitted and an eight-point roll cage keeps competitors safe.

Races last around forty-five minutes and the series visits world-famous circuits like Laguna Seca, Sebring and Road America, supporting other high-profile SCCA Pro Racing Series. As such, the Playboy MX-5 Cup is the pinnacle of single-make MX-5 racing.

MAX5 (UK)

The MaX5 Racing series, with the slogan 'Taking Fun Seriously', is similar in ethos to the Spec Miata series in the US, with tightly controlled rules and classes for different generations of MX-5. Started in summer 2003 by Alyn Robson and Jonathan Halliwell, the series was initially based on the original Spec Miata series that ran in the US shortly after the MX-5 was launched, in 1990-1991.

The series was originally open to 1.6-litre MX-5s and imported Eunos Roadsters, but now includes the increasingly popular Mk3 model too, in 1.8 and 2.0-litre capacities. Whichever car the driver chooses, the bodyshell, engine and transmission must all remain standard, and the majority of modifications required by the series organisers are to increase safety. A full FIA-approved seven-point roll cage has been specially developed for the series. Cars must also include a fully plumbed-in fire extinguisher system and a single race seat with a five-point safety harness. Each class runs a control alloy wheel design from Team Dynamics or Rota, race-spec brake pads (though discs and callipers remain road-standard) and a Hankook or Federal control tyre. Unlike the series' American counterpart, all cars run as open vehicles, rather than using the factory hard top.

All prospective racers are required to join the MaX5 Racing Club and British Automobile Racing Club (BARC), and a National B ARDS licence is needed to compete in the series. Rounds are held at circuits across the UK, including Anglesey, Brands Hatch, Croft, Mallory Park, Pembrey and Snetterton. Some of these rounds are double-headers, with two races at the same meeting. Races typically last around twenty minutes.

Class A is open to the original 1.6-litre MX-5 and Eunos Roadster. Minimum weight is 970kg (2,138lb) and engine modification is tightly controlled. Class B is open to Mk3

MX-5s of 1.8 and 2.0-litres in capacity, and some modification is allowed – aftermarket manifolds and exhaust back boxes and, on the 1.8, higher-lift camshafts. Suspension type is restricted on Mk1 cars, but free on Mk3s, though there are ride height, anti-roll bar and strut brace restrictions on both classes. Class B cars also have to run to a minimum weight of 1100kg (2,425lb).

Ever popular, the series' profile has been boosted in recent years by TV coverage and every race is now shown in the UK on digital TV channel MotorsTV.

JOTA SPORT MX-5 GT

While single-model series dominate the MX-5 racing scene, UK-based Jota Sport has developed possibly the ultimate MX-5 racecar, in order to compete in the Avon Tyres British GT Championship. Built to race against Lotus, Nissan, BMW and Aston Martin cars in the British GT Championship's GT4 class, the Jota Sport MX-5 GT was commissioned by Mazda UK in 2010, as part of the MX-5's 21st anniversary. The result is a highly tuned car with more than 1,500 man hours invested in its design and development – 400 hours on the engine alone.

Jota Sport minimised weight while maximising power and the racers use a 2.0-litre engine derived from that of the standard car. However, with several modifications and forced induction, the tuned unit produces 320hp at 7,000 rpm – twice that of the standard car. Torque rises to 350Nm (258lb ft) at 6,000 rpm. The gearbox changes are even more pronounced, with a six-speed sequential dog-type (non-synchromesh) gearbox. A limited-slip differential helps send power to the rear wheels.

Much of the exterior bodywork remains standard, but the car gains a carbon fibre front splitter and functional rear diffuser, and a race-suitable polycarbonate windscreen replaces the standard glass item. Suspension is double-wishbone all round, replacing the rear multi-link from the road car, and uses Ohlins coil-over springs and dampers, with anti-roll bars. Four-piston callipers on floating discs, with a twin master-cylinder pedal box handle the braking. The large discs sit behind one-piece 17in alloy wheels.

Given the car's high standard of development, it was no surprise that success was soon achieved. The British GT round at Brands Hatch saw the MX-5 score a third place finish in GT4, in the hands of Mark Ticehurst and Owen

Green and mean, Jota Sport's GT4 MX-5 has shown podium potential. JOTA SPORT

The MX-5 GT4 car has competed successfully in the British GT Championship. JOTA SPORT

Mildenhall. After a brief rain shower, the car even held second place overall for a few laps, fending off larger Ferraris, Porsches and Mercedes from the GT3 class.

Following a positive reception at the 2012 Goodwood Festival of Speed, where a road going, Jota-developed MX-5 GT Concept was launched, the team also scored a second place finish at Snetterton. Potential racers with the necessary £125,000 can buy their own GT.

Alternative Motor Sports

A beauty of the MX-5 is that, despite the wealth of single-make series dedicated to the model, it can be raced almost anywhere that an enthusiastic owner sees fit. This means that MX-5s have competed in every discipline from auto testing, through drift competitions and hill climbs to rallying.

Auto testing and autocross are popular beginner motor sports ideally suited to the Mazda MX-5. Both are timed events involving precision driving between cones in large, empty spaces. This means fewer hard objects to hit, short, frequent runs that allow both car and driver to cool down and compose themselves, and a friendly atmosphere.

Auto testing is a little slower than autocross and often features a highly technical cone course with slalom sections, figure eights and reversing stages. Competitors are timed and judged on accuracy; contact with cones incurs penalties. Autocross is similar, but usually involves faster driving over a cone course, akin to a small tarmac rally stage. Drivers are once again timed and penalised for hitting cones. Both forms of motor sport are ideal for beginners and the MX-5 alike. The car's nimble handling and rear-wheel drive allow beginners to learn the basics of car control, and MX-5s are cheap and competitive, making both disciplines an inexpensive way to start out in motor-

sport. The MX-5 is also the ideal car when it comes to upgrading for improved performance. A huge aftermarket for parts, plus inherently simple mechanicals, makes the MX-5 almost perfect for the home mechanic. It's also useful in the event of an accident...

The MX-5 also makes a competitive hill climb car. Several hill courses around the UK hold events and entry fees are usually less than £100, plus membership of the club running the event. As with auto-testing and autocross, tuning the car is not usually necessary, unless one wishes to compete in a higher class. Unmodified sub-1.6 and sub-2.0 classes are common, which covers every generation of MX-5. Hill climb courses are often a little faster than autocross venues and their narrow tracks require plenty of skill to navigate quickly. When drivers get it wrong, there are usually more obstacles to hit too! The lack of wheel-to-wheel competition and set specification rules again make this a fairly inexpensive way into motor sport and a standard MX-5 should be both competitive and fun to drive.

MX-5s are not restricted to tarmac events of course. They may seem like an odd choice for a rally car, but several owners worldwide have taken their cars off the straight and narrow. With perfect weight distribution and a lightweight chassis, the MX-5 is actually quite suited to off-road racing. Those planning on doing similar may wish to stiffen the chassis and virtually all rally organisers will require that a competing car has a roof.

Perhaps a more suitable alternative motor sport for the MX-5, therefore, is drifting. In a discipline that mixes car control, precision and style, Mazda's rear-drive roadster already has the ideal setup. Its short wheelbase can make the MX-5 a little tricky on the limit, particularly given the extra power the car requires to hold longer drifts, but as one of the cheaper and more reliable rear-wheel drive cars on the market, it is a popular choice for beginners to the sport.

CHAPTER 17

WHAT DOES THE FUTURE HOLD?

As Mazda's designers and engineers discovered when the company launched the Mk3 MX-5, redesigning an icon is no easy task. Unlike most new models, which are simply expected to evolve into more rounded and useful products, gaining comfort, equipment and safety, an MX-5 also needs to match its predecessors in less tangible categories. Only then will increased levels of comfort, equipment and safety be said to improve the vehicle as an MX-5, rather than just as a vehicle.

In the short term, Mazda has confirmed that it will continue building the NC-generation (Mk3) MX-5. Mid-2012 saw leaked images of a facelifted Japanese Mazda Roadster hit the internet, sporting a redesigned front end. The updated car used a new five-point front grille, with a more curved upper section. The fog lamp surrounds appeared larger and more aggressive, and black units replaced the silver headlamp bezels. The altered styling has made the car more aerodynamically efficient.

New alloy wheels and colour options are also available. Mazda unveiled the new car in full at the 2012 Paris Auto Show and it went on sale in the UK in December 2012. Exterior changes from the existing Mk3.5 are subtle, but notable is a new pedestrian-friendly bonnet design. The 'active bonnet' detects a pedestrian impact and its trailing edge rises, putting more space between the bonnet, pedestrian and hard engine components below. Such systems are designed to reduce the risk of head injury should the worst happen. The re-designed front bumper has also been re-profiled to reduce leg injury in pedestrian impact.

A new colour, Dolphin Grey Mica, was made available. The interior also sees subtle changes, with more black trim giving the cockpit a slightly more grown-up, upmarket feel. A large central touch-screen adds to this impression, while the option of Recaro sport seats is available.

To keep the model competitive, Mazda introduced subtle updates in 2012. MAZDA

Meeting the challenge of new rivals like the Toyota GT 86, Mazda has also re-worked the car's driveability. Throttle pedal response on the manual transmission models has been improved and the car is now more responsive at lower engine speeds. The vacuum brake booster has also been revised, enhancing braking feel. The transition between increased response of brakes and throttle gives MX-5 drivers even more control and secures Mazda's 'Jinba Ittai' ethos for another few years.

Rumours abound as to what the next generation MX-5 will be like, but it could be 2015 before the next model is released. Even so, Mazda's current design and engineering directions point towards how the car may look and what engines it might use. A series of sophisticated concepts launched at major motor shows has begun to influence the company's production line up, and a new range

The Shinari Concept was the first expression of Mazda's 'Kodo – soul of motion' design language. MAZDA

of powerplants under the SKYACTIV brand name will eventually see use throughout the entire Mazda offering.

September 2010 saw the unveiling of the Mazda Shinari concept car at a private viewing in Milan. A long, sleek saloon, its styling matched any super saloon on sale at the time, drawing comparison with the Aston Martin Rapide and Mercedes-Benz CLS for its coupé-like roofline and sporting attributes. More significantly, the five-point front grille, sharply detailed headlights and flowing flanks were part of a new Mazda design language, replacing the short-lived 'Nagare' style. Known as 'Kodo', translated as 'soul of motion', the new concept was designed to blend sup-pleness with tension – the lines bringing to mind the effects of a sheet pulled over a more defined form.

The Kodo ideals became further developed at the 2011 Geneva Motor Show, with the launch of another concept vehicle. Known as the Minagi, the concept previewed the look of a new small crossover vehicle that eventually became the CX-5 production car. Less beautiful than the Shinari, the Minagi nevertheless shared similar forms, with a confident grille, strong front arches, a sleek roofline and sides that appeared to flow organically. Many of these cues made it to the CX-5 unhindered and shortly after the CX-5's launch at the 2011 Frankfurt Motor Show, Mazda used the 2012 Geneva Motor Show to display yet another Kodo concept.

The Takeri was, to all intents and purposes, the next Mazda6 family car. Longer, sleeker and more purposeful,

Minagi paved the way for another Kodo-inspired car, the CX-5 crossover. MAZDA

it was also the boldest expression of the new design language and few were surprised that the eventual production car, launched in autumn 2012, differed little from the concept. It would also be of little surprise if the next MX-5 adopted many Kodo features, carefully integrated into a shape that does not stray too far from the ideas of what an MX-5 should be. Speaking in 2010, Mazda's Chief Designer, Peter Birtwhistle, gave his opinions on how one should recognise an MX-5, and the challenges of designing the next generation.

To Birtwhistle, an MX-5 should have: 'A simple, basic body shape with mostly parallel-running lines… these lines do not form points, do not have any dramatically crossing edges, no gimmicks.' He also notes the subtle wheel well mouldings of each generation – only pushed a little with the Mk3's flared wheel arches – while each generation of MX-5 is also defined by a slightly indented bonnet bulge, a feature likely to remain on the Mk4 car. Birtwhistle also notes his favourite feature of the MX-5, the lower front air intake and its relationship with the headlamps – the 'signature of the design.' Keeping that design signature and the car's character, when Kodo is itself such a distinctive ethos, will no doubt be a challenge.

Design is not the only aspect of the new car, however. Also previewed in 2011's Minagi concept was a new generation of Mazda engines. Known as SKYACTIV, the units were Mazda's answer to the increasing push towards efficiency in the automotive market. Ever-decreasing greenhouse gas targets and tightening pollution regulations are changing the face of the automotive landscape, and all cars – even sports cars like the MX-5 – are required to adapt.

SKYACTIV is a range of petrol and diesel engines, and manual and automatic transmissions. All were designed from the outset with engineered-in efficiency and performance, and have since raised some of Mazda's production vehicles to the top of their class in terms of fuel efficiency and emissions. Petrol engines, under the SKYACTIV-G designation, feature direct fuel injection and a high 14:1 compression ratio. Induction and exhaust cycles have been designed to reduce engine knock that is common at higher compressions.

Currently engineered in 2.0-litre and 1.3-litre capacities, the SKYACTIV-G range is likely to grow further and inevitably a variant of the SKYACTIV range will be used in the next-generation MX-5 – possibly with a turbocharger, ensuring performance matches the current car.

Mazda's line of SKYACTIV engines is designed to maximise performance and minimise fuel consumption. MAZDA

Under the wider banner of SKYACTIV Technology, Mazda is also working on its next generation of lightweight bodies. Several of Mazda's recent models have been lighter than their predecessors, and in 2008 Mazda claimed that the next-generation MX-5 would weigh under 1,000kg (2,205lb). That's a reduction of 120kg (265lb) on the Mk3 and dips beneath a barrier not seen since the first-generation MX-5 was released back in 1989. Mazda also said that alloy use would be minimal, owing to its cost, so steel is likely to be the primary construction material. Mazda2 levels of fuel efficiency and emissions are also a target, implying CO2 emissions in the 120g/km region.

Advanced Competition

The competition for Mazda's next roadster could be fierce. Subaru and Toyota's lightweight sports cars, the BRZ and GT-86, are likely to increase the popularity of back-to-basics performance cars, an arena ruled largely by Mazda and the MX-5 for several years. Even closer to the next MX-5 will be Alfa Romeo's next-generation Spider. Indeed, May 2012 saw Mazda and Alfa Romeo embark upon a joint venture in which Alfa Romeo gets sports car building expertise not available from its parent, Fiat, and Mazda benefits from the Fiat group's deep pockets to help it finance development.

A 20th anniversary celebration in Japan brought cars and owners from far and wide. Will the next-generation MX-5 have such a following? MAZDA

The resulting cars will have unique styling, interiors, engines and transmissions, but the basic underpinnings will be very similar. Alfa Romeo's version is likely to draw inspiration from the original 1966 Duetto Spider and more recent models, while the Mazda will likely display both Kodo and classic MX-5 touches. The Alfa Romeo is likely to be more expensive, but if the Italian car's styling is just right, Mazda may find it no longer controls the roadster market.

Whatever the future holds for the Mazda MX-5, there's little doubt that a successful reinterpretation will continue to keep the model at the forefront for those who wish to drive an inexpensive and uncomplicated sports car. New models may gain more equipment, offer greater comfort and deliver greater levels of safety, but the MX-5 has an essentially simple formula.

Its next incarnation will combine an adjustable front-engined, rear-drive chassis. It will use small, efficient engines to deliver just enough performance for fun driving, while meeting the latest fuel economy and pollution regulations. It will seat two and provide adequate luggage space, but retain classic sports car proportions. And, above all, it will be affordable. All those facets are key to the MX-5's enduring appeal and deviating from such a formula would not only be harmful to the car, but harmful to Mazda itself. As the MX-5 heads towards its quarter century, it remains the backbone of the Mazda range, a car from which all other Mazdas take their spirit.

INDEX